grades

Day-by-Day MATH PLANS

A Week's Worth of Ideas for Each of **24** Skills

- Learning centers
- Group-time activities
- Project-time activities
- Gross-motor practice
- Transition activities
- Snacks

- Songs and rhymes
- Take-home activities
- Time fillers
- Patterns and practice pages

Plus 12 handy math teaching aids!

Managing Editor: Kimberly Ann Brugger

Editorial Team: Becky S. Andrews, Diane Badden, Tricia Kylene Brown, Kimberley Bruck, Karen A. Brudnak, Elizabeth Cook, Pam Crane, Chris Curry, David Drews, Ada Goren, Tazmen Fisher Hansen, Erica Haver, Marsha Heim, Lori Z. Henry, Brenda Fay, Mark Rainey, Greg D. Rieves, Mary Robles, Hope Rodgers-Medina, Rebecca Saunders, Donna K. Teal, Sharon M. Tresino, Zane Williard

www.themailbox.com

©2013 The Mailbox® Books
All rights reserved.
ISBN 978-1-61276-257-9

Printed in the United States
10 9 8 7 6 5 4 3 2 1

HPS246106

What's Inside

Each math skill includes

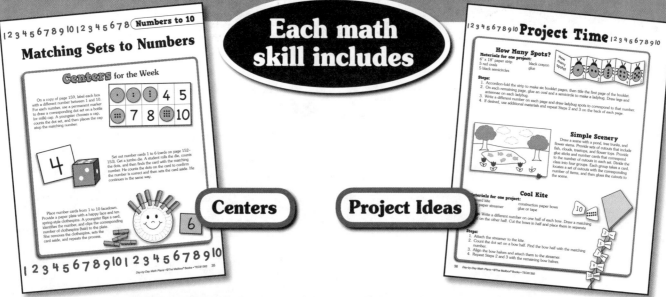

Centers

Project Ideas

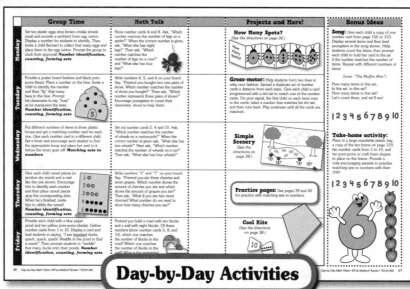

Day-by-Day Activities

Two Ready-to-Copy Pages

Plus 12 additional pages of math teaching aids that include

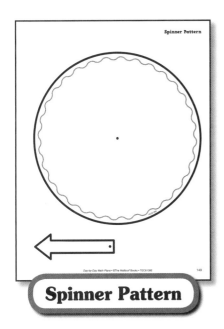

Spinner Pattern

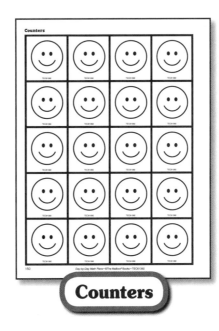

Counters

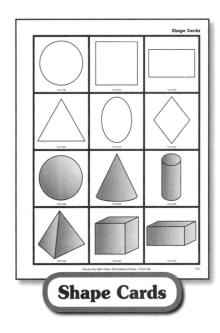

Shape Cards

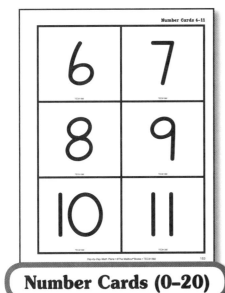

Number Cards (0–20)

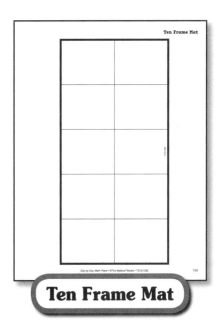

Sorting Mats

Ten Frame Mat

FREE Online Extras! Go to www.themailbox.com

Table of Contents

The kindergarten skills in this book align to **Common Core State Standards**.
www.themailbox.com/core

Color Concepts

Centers for the Week

Provide different-color nest cutouts along with corresponding color pom-poms (birds). A child takes a bird and helps it fly to a matching nest. Naming the color of the bird, he chants, "Fly, little [blue] bird, to your nest! Now sit down and take a rest!" as he maneuvers the bird.

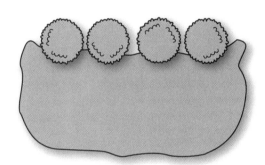

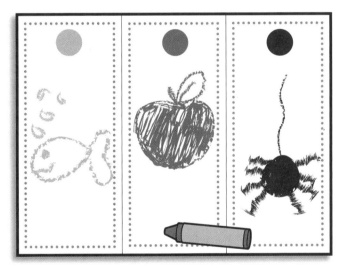

Make copies of page 157. On each copy, attach a different-color sticky dot to each section. Provide crayons to match the dots. A student chooses a dot, locates the matching-color crayon, and then uses it to draw a picture in that section.

Collect an even set of identical bottle caps. For each pair of caps, attach matching-color sticky dots, making each pair different from the others. Spread the caps dot side down. A student flips two caps. If the dots match, he sets the caps aside. If not, he turns them back over. He continues until all the caps are matched.

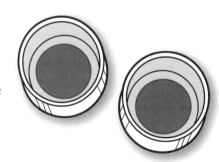

	Group Time	Math Talk
Monday	Display colorful objects. Invite a child (Captain Color) to wear a cape. Announce a color and prompt Captain Color to "fly" to the display and bring back an item that has the designated color. Then ask the group to verify whether the color is correct. Repeat with different students. **Color recognition**	Imagine you are in the produce aisle at a grocery store. What colors of fruits and vegetables might you see? Can you name some produce items and tell their colors? What fruits and vegetables can you name that are the same color?
Tuesday	Post a cake cutout. Gather self-adhesive craft foam flowers in a variety of colors. Show a flower and have the group identify its color. Then invite a child to attach the flower to the cake. Repeat with the remaining flowers. Then review each color and have students name other things of that color. **Color identification**	According to their colors, if you have a strawberry, a pear, and a tomato, which item does not belong in the group? Why? Which item does not belong if you have a lemon, a banana, and a cherry? Which item does not belong if you have a cotton ball, snow, and mud?
Wednesday	Seat students in a circle. Announce a color name, prompting each child wearing that color to stand. Repeat the process with a different color. If a student who is already standing is wearing that color also, he remains standing. If not, he sits down. Continue until everyone has had the opportunity to stand. **Color recognition**	What if your friend told you she saw a real cow with purple spots. Do you think this would be true? Why? What about a pink duck? Why? A blue pig? Why? A green horse? Why?
Thursday	Place colorful objects in a sack. For each color, place a matching sheet of construction paper on the floor. Invite youngsters, in turn, to draw an item from the sack. Ask students to identify the object's color; then have the child place the item on the matching paper. **Color identification, matching, and sorting**	Colors can make you feel different ways. What color makes you feel [emotion]? Why?
Friday	Display a pattern of colorful circles. Put matching circles in a bag. Play music and have students pass the bag. Stop the music and have the child with the bag remove a circle and tell the color. If that color begins the pattern, he places the circle below the pattern. If not, he returns it to the bag. Continue to complete the pattern. **Color identification and patterning**	We can usually tell the weather according to colors we see outdoors. What do you think the weather will be if the sky is blue? What if you see a few white clouds? What about gray clouds?

Projects and More!

Colorful Suncatcher
(See the directions on page 8.)

Gross Motor: Arrange chairs in a circle. Place a paper scrap under each chair, making sure to have two of each color. Have youngsters walk around the circle. Clap your hands and prompt each child to sit in a chair and remove the paper. Have students find a classmate with the matching paper, switch places with them, and then put the paper under that chair. Continue for several rounds.

Fancy Flag
(See the directions on page 8.)

Practice pages: See pages 9 and 10 for practice with color concepts.

Dip and Dab
(See the directions on page 8.)

Bonus Ideas

Time filler: Engage youngsters in a game of "I Spy Colors" using these fun rhyming cues!

I spy something blue. Can you do it too?
I spy something red. Red is what I said!
I spy something green. Yes, green can be seen!
I spy something pink. What do you think?
I spy something brown. Look up and look down!

Transition activity: This idea is perfect for introducing color hues! Obtain several paint strips, making sure each color collection is clearly different from the others. Cut apart the strips. Display one section from each strip and place the remaining cards in a bag. Ask a child to take a "paint chip" from the bag and place it with a corresponding color card. Then send him on his way!

Project Time

Colorful Suncatcher

Materials for one project:

clear adhesive covering cut in a rainbow shape
cotton batting
tissue paper squares in rainbow colors

Setup:

Use a permanent marker to draw arcs on the rainbow cutout. Then peel off the backing and position the rainbow on a table, sticky-side up.

Steps:

1. Press appropriate colors of the tissue paper on each arc.
2. Attach cotton batting clouds to the rainbow.
3. Display the rainbow in a sunny window.

Fancy Flag

Materials for one project:

white felt rectangle	assorted stampers
fabric or tempera paint	paint stirrer
paper plate for each color of paint	hot-glue gun *(for teacher use)*

Steps:

1. Put a thin layer of paint on individual plates.
2. Press a stamper in the paint and then on the felt.
3. Repeat Step 2 using other stampers and colors of paint. *(Tip: If using the same stamper in a different color of paint, clean the stamper with a wipe or wet paper towel first.)*
4. When the paint is dry, hot-glue the felt to the paint stirrer to make a flag.

Dip and Dab

For this colorful process art, crumple a sheet of aluminum foil, molding part of it to create a handle. Make several of these foil paint tools and provide a different color of paint for each one. Invite a child to dip a foil tool in paint and then dab it on a sheet of paper, adding more paint to the foil as needed. Encourage her to repeat the process with other foil painters and colors of paint. When the paint is dry, mount the project on contrasting color paper.

Name _____

Playtime for Froggy!

All About Frogs

Day-by-Day Math Plans • ©The Mailbox® Books • TEC61392

Note to the teacher: Instruct the student to color the ball red, the truck brown, the duck orange, the bear blue, the book yellow, the drum purple, and the frogs green.

Name _____

Giant Gumballs

Color by the code.

Color Code			
1	2	3	4
◯	◯	◯	◯
red	blue	green	yellow

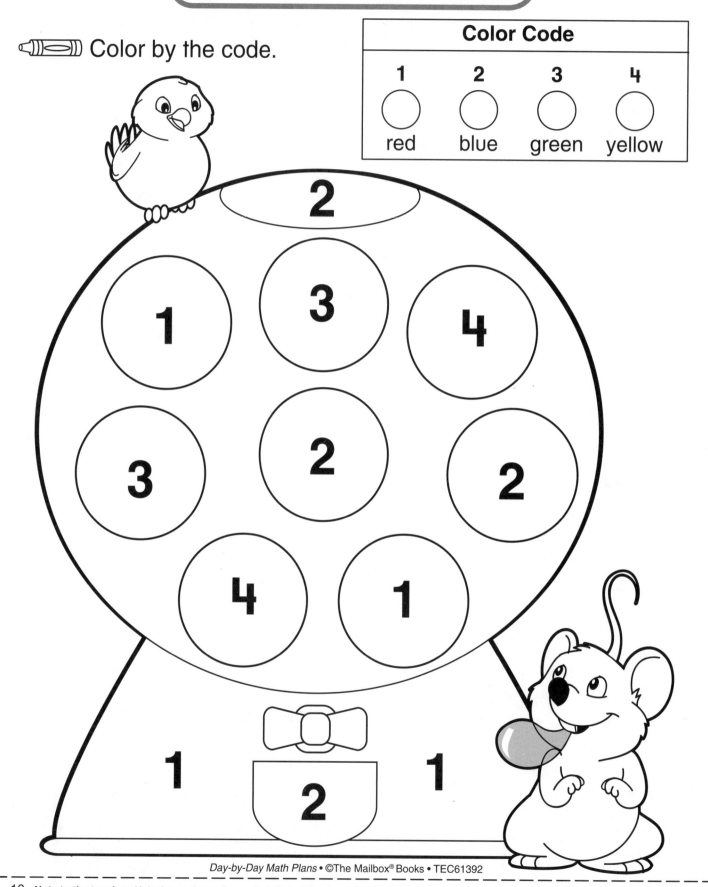

Note to the teacher: Help the student color each circle in the color code; then have him use the code to color the picture.

One-to-One Correspondence

Centers for the Week

Glue ice cream cone cutouts to cardboard. Provide an ice cream scooper and large pom-poms (ice cream scoops). A youngster uses the scooper to put one ice cream scoop atop each cone. Then he counts the cones, saying one number name for each cone he counts.

Provide library pockets (sleeping bags) and an equal number of craft sticks programmed with faces (people camping). A student counts the sleeping bags and then counts the people. Then he places one camper in each sleeping bag.

Set out clown head cutouts (pattern on page 15) and pom-poms (noses). A child counts the clown heads and counts the noses. Then she places one nose on each clown face.

	Group Time	Math Talk
Monday	Put a few manipulatives in a lidded container. Shake the container as youngsters chant, "Shake it up, shake it up! Spill them out!" Remove the lid and spill the items. Then have students count each item as you point to it. Repeat with different numbers of items. ***Counting with one-to-one correspondence***	To paint a picture using three different colors of paint, how many paintbrushes will you need? Explain. What if you added another color of paint?
Tuesday	Set out stuffed toy dogs (or dog cutouts). Invite a child to give a bone cutout to one dog as the group chants, "Little doggy, oh so sweet. Here's a bone for you to eat!" Repeat with other students until each dog has a bone. ***Pairing objects with one-to one correspondence***	Imagine a friend and you go to the park and see two empty swings. Will each of you be able to swing? Why? What if another friend shows up? Will there be enough swings? What could you do?
Wednesday	Get five beanbags. Place five paper plates in your circle. Play music and have youngsters pass a beanbag around the circle. Stop the music and have the child holding the beanbag put it on a plate as the group chants, "One beanbag on one plate!" Repeat until each plate has a beanbag. ***Pairing objects with one-to-one correspondence***	If five children attend a birthday party, how many birthday hats are needed? Explain. What if only four children come to the party?
Thursday	Place several chairs facing the group. Have a group of students stand. Count the chairs. Then count the students. Lead students in guiding one child to each chair, noticing whether there are too many chairs or too many students and using the words *more* and *fewer* in their discussion. ***Counting with one-to-one correspondence, comparing sets***	Imagine there are four baby birds in a nest. To feed each baby one worm, how many worms will the mommy bird need to find? What do you think worms taste like?
Friday	Lay plastic hoops (nests) on the floor. Ask, "If one chicken sat in each nest, how many chickens would there be?" After confirming an answer, invite one student (chicken) to sit in each nest. Ask, "If each chicken laid one egg, how many eggs would there be?" Give each chicken a plastic egg. Review how each grouping has one hoop, one chicken, and one egg. ***Grouping with one-to-one correspondence***	Pretend you bake six chocolate chip cookies. The recipe says to top each cookie with a candy kiss. How many candy kisses do you need? What if you had an extra candy kiss? What would you do?

Projects and More!

Dot-to-Dot Booklet
(See the directions on page 14.)

Partner activity:
Set out disposable cups and provide a different number of craft sticks. Encourage each child to predict whether there are more cups or craft sticks, or if the amounts are the same. Then have them work together placing one stick in each cup to see if their predictions are correct.

Sweet Sprinkles
(See the directions on page 14.)

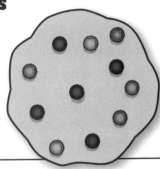

Practice page:
See page 16 for practice with one-to-one correspondence.

Pepperoni Pizza
(See the directions on page 14.)

Bonus Ideas

Time filler:
Program tagboard strips with different numbers of pompoms and place the strips in a bag. Randomly draw a strip from the bag. Then point to each pom-pom, prompting youngsters to count aloud as you point. Return the strip to the bag and repeat the activity as time allows.

Song:
Practice counting one to one with this whole-group activity! Seat youngsters in a circle and lead them in the song shown. Then walk around the circle and tap each child on the head, prompting the group to count along.

(tune: "Mary Had a Little Lamb")

Counting can be so much fun,
So much fun, so much fun.
Counting can be so much fun
When counting one to one!

Project Time

Dot-to-Dot Booklet

With this booklet project, students practice counting one to one and develop fine-motor skills! Make a five-page booklet for each child, marking each page with one to five dots. For each page, instruct youngsters to place one sticky dot atop each programmed dot. Then have her count the dots on each page, encouraging her to say one number for each dot she counts.

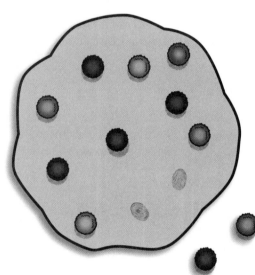

Sweet Sprinkles

Provide cookie cutouts, an ink pad, a supply of mini pom-poms (sprinkles), and glue. Instruct each child to choose a cookie. Have her press her finger on the ink pad and then on the cookie. Have her repeat the process several times; then encourage her to glue one sprinkle atop each print.

Pepperoni Pizza

What's cooking with this craft? More one-to-one fun! Give each child a triangle cutout (pizza slice). Provide brown tissue paper (crust), red craft foam circles (pepperoni), and glue. Encourage him to glue the crust to his slice. Have him count out several pieces of pepperoni, reminding him to say one number for each pepperoni. Then have him glue the pepperoni to his pizza.

TEC61392

Name _____

Swimming Along

✂ Cut. 🖊 Glue to match one to one.

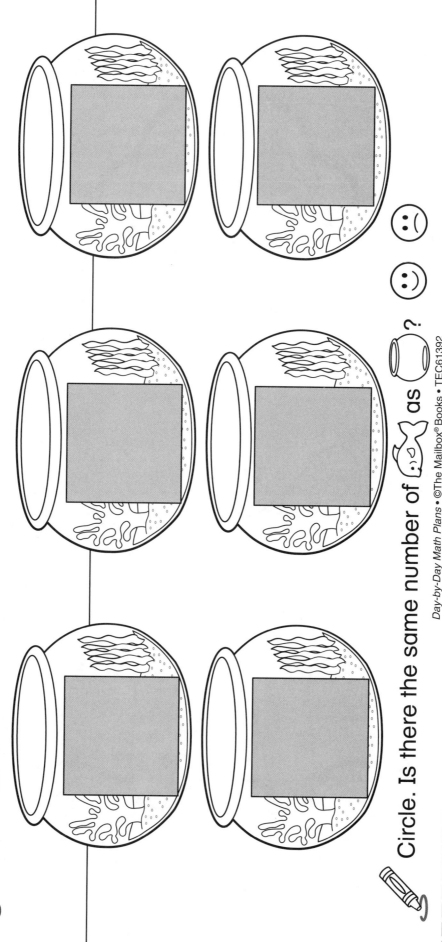

Circle. Is there the same number of 🐟 as 🐠 ?

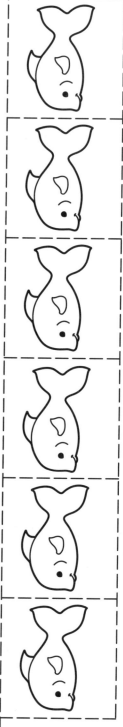

Day-by-Day Math Plans • ©The Mailbox® Books • TEC61392

16

Forming Sets

Centers for the Week

Provide school supplies such as markers, crayons, and pencils, along with a labeled container for each. A youngster chooses a pile of markers and then counts them. Next, he places them in the appropriate container. He continues with each remaining item.

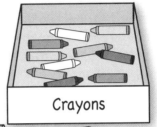
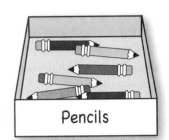

Provide a container of linking cubes. Cut a slip of paper that corresponds to each linking cube color and place the slips in a bag. A child chooses a slip of paper. Then he gathers several corresponding linking cubes into a set and builds a tower. He counts the linking cubes and then returns them to the container.

Make copies of page 156. Use a bingo dauber to stamp a dot set on one side of each page. A child takes a page and counts the dots. Then she uses a bingo dauber to duplicate the dot set on the opposite side of the page.

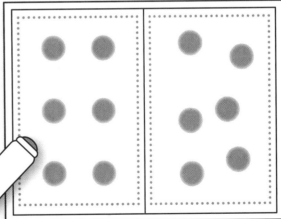

	Group Time	Math Talk	

Monday

Give each child a blue paper pond and ten fish-shaped crackers. Say, "Your pond is empty. There are no fish. Make a set of [number] go swish, swish, swish!" Then encourage each child to place that many fish on her pond. Have her remove the fish and repeat the process. **Forming sets**

Imagine you're making a necklace. You have seven beads. How many more beads do you need to have a set of ten?

Tuesday

Get a die. Provide each child with black paper (night sky) and six die-cut stars. Invite a child to roll the die and count the dots. Prompt each youngster to place that many stars in his sky; then lead students in counting the set. For more of a challenge, use two dice and give each child 12 stars. **Forming sets**

Pretend you are baking cookies and are putting cookies on a plate for your mom. How many cookies would you put on the plate? Show me how you would count out the set of cookies. How many cookies would you give your dad? Your sisters or brothers?

Wednesday

Gather several toy cars. Put two plastic hoops on the floor. Have a child place a number of cars in each hoop. Then lead youngsters in counting the number of vehicles in each set. **Forming sets**

You invite four friends to a tea party but have only two teacups. How many more cups do you need to have a set of four?

Thursday

Program a copy of the spinner on page 149 with dot sets. Use a brad to attach the arrow to the spinner. Give each child a paper plate and a set of pom-poms equal to the greatest dot set. Invite a child to spin the spinner and count the dots spun. Have each child place that many pom-poms on her plate and then count the resulting set. **Forming sets**

Name a toy you have more than one of. How many do you have?

Friday

Attach a bubble wand to a whiteboard. Hand a student a wipe-off marker. Lead the group in saying, "Blowing bubbles is fun, you know! How many bubbles will you blow?" Announce a number and prompt the child to draw that many circles above the wand. Wipe the board clean and repeat with other students. **Drawing to form sets**

How many children are in this room? How many adults? How many tables are in the room? How many chairs? How many doors?

| Projects and More! | Bonus Ideas |

Projects and More!

A Ring of Sets
(See the directions on page 20.)

Game: On a copy of the mat on page 156, glue a set of pom-poms to one half. Prepare several mats. Provide pom-poms. Set a timer. Encourage a child to count the pom-poms on the mat and then place a matching set on the blank side before the timer goes off. Continue with other mats.

Cork Print Petals
(See the directions on page 20.)

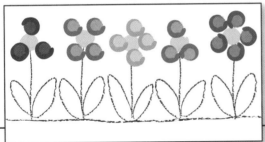

Practice pages: See pages 21 and 22 for practice with forming sets.

Scooping Sets
(See the directions on page 20.)

Bonus Ideas

Snack: Set out graham cracker halves, whipped cream cheese, and mini chocolate chips. Help each child spread cream cheese on two crackers. Have her put a designated number of chocolate chips on one cracker; then ask her to put a matching set of chips on the remaining cracker.

Song: Give each child a handful of craft sticks. Draw lines on a whiteboard, encouraging youngsters to count each line as you draw. Then sing the song shown and prompt students to duplicate the set of lines using the craft sticks.

(tune: "The Muffin Man")

Can you make a set for me,
A set for me, a set for me?
Can you make a set for me?
Show me now. Let's see!

Project Time

A Ring of Sets

This project makes it easy to practice counting sets anywhere anytime! Give each child several blank index cards. Provide ink pads and assorted stamps. Encourage her to stamp a different image and number of prints on each card. Then help her bind the cards together with a metal ring.

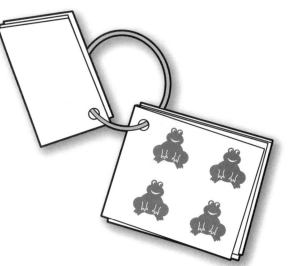

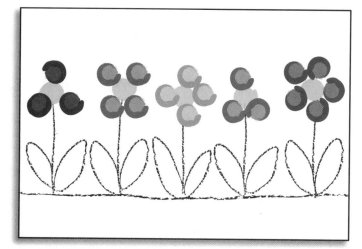

Cork Print Petals

Encourage each child to draw a set of five stems on a sheet of construction paper. Have her make a set of two leaves on each stem. Then have her dip a cork in a shallow pan of yellow paint and make a print above each stem. Next, have her make sets of colorful cork prints (petals) around the flower centers.

Scooping Sets

Make a five-page booklet for each child. Program each page with a bowl cutout and dot set from one to five. Prompt a child to count the dots on each page and then draw the same number of ice cream scoops above the bowl. Invite each child to take her booklet home to practice counting sets with her family!

Name _____

Bunches of Balloons

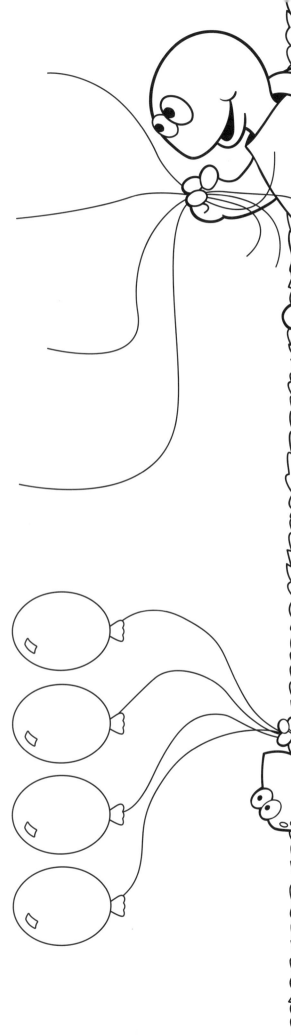

Count the 🎈.

Draw 4 🎈.

Day-by-Day Math Plans • ©The Mailbox® Books • TEC61392

Name _____

Rainy Day

 Count.

Draw to finish each set.

Day-by-Day Math Plans • ©The Mailbox® Books • TEC61392

Comparing Sets

Centers for the Week

Punch a hole in each of two plastic lids and connect them with a metal ring. Attach a different number of stickers to each lid. Make several pairs. A student chooses a pair of lids and counts the stickers on each lid to determine which set has more. For self-checking, attach a star sticker to the back of the appropriate lid.

Puzzle-cut a sheet of craft foam and use a permanent marker to draw equal dot sets on each half. Make several puzzles with different cuts and dot sets; then mix the halves. A child matches two puzzle halves. Then he counts each dot set to confirm that they are equal.

Provide a copy of page 156, a container of pasta wheels, and a large die. A youngster rolls the die, counts the dots, and places that many pasta wheels on one half of the mat. He repeats the process for the remaining half. Then he counts each set of wheels to determine which has fewer.

	Group Time	Math Talk
Monday	Make two oversize masking tape squares on the floor. Call on different numbers of students to stand in each square. Lead the group in counting the children in each square and then ask, "Which square has more (or fewer) children?" Repeat for several rounds. ***Comparing sets with more or fewer amounts***	What if you had a set of six tennis balls and a set of eight golf balls? Would the sets be equal? Explain. What could you do to make the sets equal?
Tuesday	Give each child a pipe cleaner snake (provide several colors). Say, "I hear [color] snakes hiss, hiss, hiss!" prompting children with that color to group the snakes together. Repeat with a different color. Then help students count and compare each set, using words such as *more, fewer,* and *equal to.* ***Comparing sets with more, fewer, and equal amounts***	Imagine you're at the beach collecting seashells. You collect seven white shells and ten pink shells. Which set of seashells has more and which has fewer? If you have seven white shells, how many more do you need to have a set of ten?
Wednesday	Attach different amounts of self-adhesive craft foam shapes to paint stirrers and place them in a canister. Chant, "Pretty shape sticks ready to pick. [Child's name], please come pick a stick!" Repeat to call another child. Then help students count and compare the number of shapes on each stick. Repeat. ***Counting and comparing sets***	Pretend your teacher gives you two sheets of stickers: one sheet with six large stickers and one sheet with eight small stickers. Are the sets of stickers equal or unequal? Explain.
Thursday	Set out two paper puddles and craft foam raindrops. Invite a child to stand near each puddle. Lead the group in chanting, "I hear raindrops drip, drip, drop, falling in a puddle. Plip, plip, plop!" Prompt each child to drop a handful of raindrops onto her puddle; then help students count and compare the results. ***Counting and comparing sets***	Imagine you sort recycled items. You have ten plastic bottles and ten aluminum cans. Does one set of recycling have more than the other? Explain.
Friday	Give each child laminated paper, a wipe-off marker, and a wipe. Draw a set of circles on the board. Lead students in counting the circles; then ask them to draw a set of circles equal to yours. Repeat the activity, having students draw sets that are less than and more than yours. ***Drawing and comparing sets***	Pretend your mom sets out two plates of chocolate chip cookies. One plate has five cookies and one plate has three cookies. Which plate of cookies would you want? Why?

Projects and More!

Sizing Up Sets
(See the directions on page 26.)

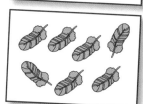

Partner activity: Place a handful of bear counters in each of two bags. Encourage each child to handle the bags and guess which has more bears, which has less bears, or if they have an equal amount. Have each child spill a bag and count the bears; then help them compare the results.

Beautiful Skyline
(See the directions on page 26.)

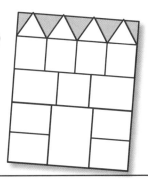

Practice pages: See pages 27 and 28 for practice with comparing sets.

Hungry Bugs
(See the directions on page 26.)

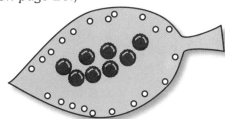

Bonus Ideas

Transition: Give each child an index card programmed with a dot set. Show a card with three dots and ask a child if her dot set has more dots, fewer dots, or the same number of dots as yours. After determining the correct answer, have her move to the next activity.

Song: Lead youngsters in the song shown, prompting children to hold up the named amount of fingers on each hand. At the end of the song, help students compare the number of fingers displayed using words such as *more, fewer,* and *equal to.*

(tune: "Where Is Thumbkin?")

Show [number] fingers,
Show [number] fingers
On this hand,
On this hand.
Now hold up [number] fingers,
Now hold up [number] fingers
On this hand,
On this hand.

Project Time

Sizing Up Sets

This crafty project enhances artistic expression and comparison skills! Post a paper programmed with five craft feathers. Mount near the paper three labels that say "more than," "less than," and "equal to." Then invite each child to glue craft feathers to a sheet of construction paper. Help him count the feathers and then post his project under the appropriate label.

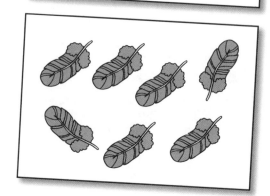

Beautiful Skyline

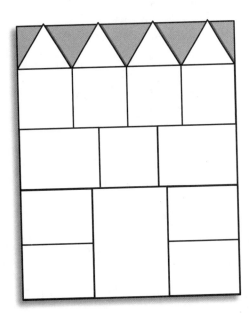

Divide the class into small groups. For each group, provide a large sheet of construction paper, construction paper shapes, and glue. Encourage students to glue shapes to the paper so the design resembles a building. Then mount the projects on a wall beside one another. Help youngsters count and compare the number of shapes used to create each building.

Hungry Bugs

Materials for one project:
green leaf cutout
colorful pom-poms (bugs)
hole puncher
glue

Steps:
1. Punch holes near the edge of the leaf. Count the holes.
2. Count out a set of bugs that is equal to the number of holes.
3. Glue the bugs to the middle of the leaf.
4. Count the holes and bugs to confirm that the sets are equal.

Name

Darling Ducklings

Listen and do.

Note to the teacher: Ask a child to count each set of ducks. Help her decide which set has more ducks; then encourage her to color that set.

27

Yummy Jelly Beans

 Count.

Draw a set that is **greater**.

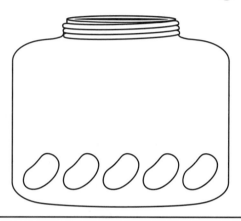 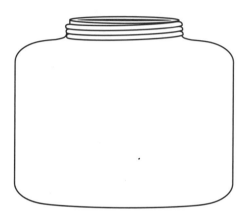

Draw a set that is **equal to**.

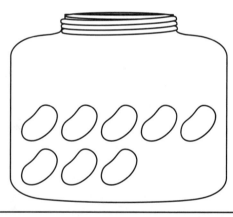 

Draw a set that is **less**.

 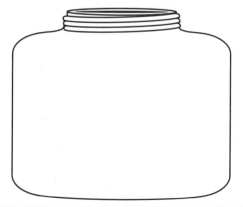

Day-by-Day Math Plans • ©The Mailbox® Books • TEC61392

Number Identification

Centers for the Week

Glue die-cut numbers to a sheet of poster board and place a matching set of numbers in a bag. A child takes a number from the bag, identifies it, and then places it atop the matching number on the board.

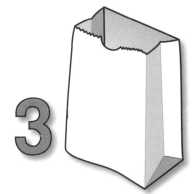

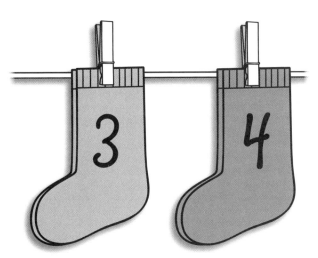

Label pairs of sock cutouts with numbers from 1 to 10. Place half of each pair in one pile and the rest in another pile. String a clothesline. Provide clothespins. A student takes a sock and identifies the number. Then he finds the sock with the matching number and hangs the pair on the line. For more of a challenge, have him hang the pairs in numerical order.

Draw several trees on bulletin board paper. Label each tree with a different number. For each tree, label several bird cutouts (patterns on page 33) with the matching number. A student takes a bird and identifies the number. She helps the bird "fly" to the appropriate tree and then repeats the process.

	Group Time	Math Talk
Monday	Label a class supply of cards with several different numbers. Give each child a card. Display a number that matches a card and chant, "See this number? What's its name? Hold yours up if it's the same!" Play several rounds. *Identifying and matching numbers*	Point to the 6 on a clock and have students identify the number. Ask, "What is something you might be doing at six in the evening?" Repeat with other numbers and times of day.
Tuesday	Try this numerical twist on Duck, Duck, Goose! Place number cards (pages 152 and 153) facedown. As a child taps his classmates, he says, "Letter, letter, number." When he says "number," the child who gets tapped flips a card and identifies the numeral. Then he becomes the "tapper." *Identifying numbers, participating in a game* Letter, letter, number!	Use a ruler to draw a ten-inch line on chart paper. Before removing the ruler, point to the 10 and help youngsters identify it. Then ask, "Can you name something that might be ten inches long like this line?" Repeat with other numbers up to nine.
Wednesday	Draw a simple TV on your board. Give each student a remote control cutout (pattern on page 33). Ask a child to name her favorite show and then pretend to turn it on by identifying a number on her remote and pressing the button. Prompt her classmates to say and press the number. Then write the number on the TV screen so youngsters can see if they pressed the right button! *Identifying numbers*	Point to the 5 on a timer and ask students to identify the number. Start the timer and prompt each child to name something they could do in five minutes. Repeat with the number 10.
Thursday	Label die-cut animals with numbers, making the numbers different on each one. Cut the animals in two and give one half to each child. Ask students to pair up with the child who has the matching half. Then have the partners identify the number and act out the animal! *Matching and identifying numbers*	Display a number and have children identify it. Ask the group to name a corresponding number of things they like to do at school. If desired, repeat with a different number and location or season.
Friday	For each student, label a sheet of paper with a number. Arrange the papers in a circle on the floor. Play music as youngsters walk around the circle. Stop the music and have each child stand near a paper; then prompt him to identify the number. Repeat for several rounds. *Identifying numbers* 4	On a calendar, point to a number between 3 and 8 for youngsters to identify. Then say, "If you count back two spaces, what number is in that box?" After the correct number is given, say, "If you count forward four spaces, what number is in that box?" Continue as desired.

Projects and More!

Awesome Alien
(See the directions on page 32.)

Partner activity: Provide playing cards (minus the face cards and aces). One child holds the deck and flips a card. The first child to identify the number keeps the card. Play continues until all the cards are flipped. Each youngster counts his cards; then the partner takes a turn to flip the cards.

Nice Web!
(See the directions on page 32.)

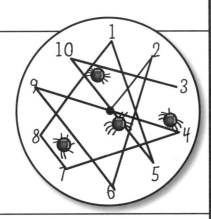

Practice page: See page 34 for practice with number identification.

Strawberry Seeds
(See directions on page 32.)

Bonus Ideas

Transition: Invite each child to wear a tagboard number bracelet throughout the day. When it's time to line up or move to a different activity, display a number for students to identify. Then send each child wearing that number on her way!

1 2 3 4 5 6 7 8 9 10

Time filler: Instruct youngsters to close their eyes while you post a number. Then chant, "There's a number hanging about. If you see it, give a shout!" Prompt students to open their eyes and look for the number. The first child to spot it calls out, "I see number [number]!" Repeat with other numbers.

1 2 3 4 5 6 7 8 9 10

Project Time

Awesome Alien

Display five cards labeled 1 to 5, each programmed with the corresponding number of craft foam shapes. Provide a supply of craft foam shapes that correspond to each card. Give each student a person cutout (alien). Have him identify the number on a card and attach that many of the designated shape to the alien. Repeat with the remaining cards; then invite him to add crayon details to the alien.

Nice Web!

Materials for one project:
tagboard circle
marker
pom-poms (spiders)
glue

Setup: Write the numbers 1 to 10 around the *edge* of the circle. Draw a dot on the circle as a starting point. Stack corresponding number cards in random order facedown.

Steps:
1. Turn over a card and identify the number.
2. Draw a line from the starting point to that number.
3. Repeat Steps 1 and 2 with the remaining cards (drawing a line from each previous number, not the starting point).
4. Randomly choose a card and identify the number. Glue that many spiders to the web.
5. Use the marker to add legs to the spiders.

Strawberry Seeds

Provide red strawberry-shaped cutouts, black paint, round-end toothpicks, green paper leaves, and glue. Show a number card and ask students to identify it. Then have each child dip a toothpick in paint and dab it on a strawberry that many times to make seeds. Repeat the process with other numbers; then encourage youngsters to glue leaves to their projects.

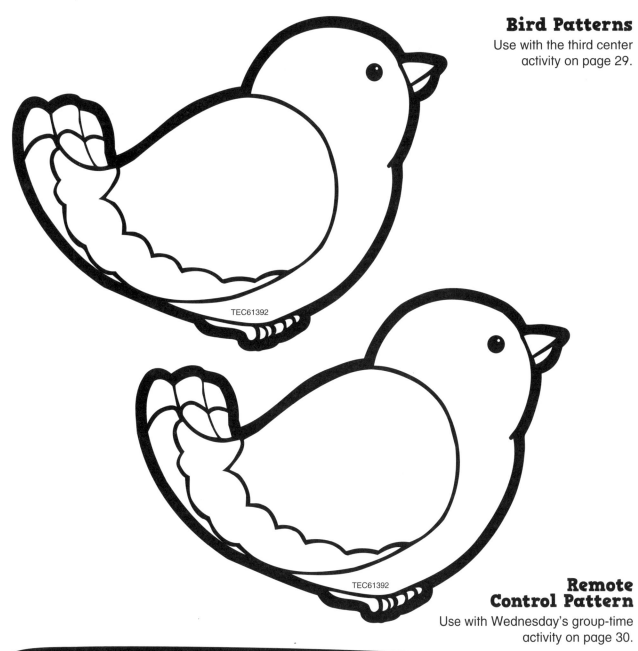

Bird Patterns

Use with the third center
activity on page 29.

TEC61392

TEC61392

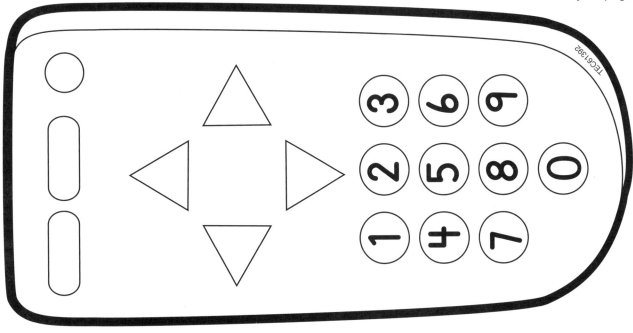

Remote
Control Pattern

Use with Wednesday's group-time
activity on page 30.

TEC61392

Name _____

Beautiful Blossoms

Listen and do.

Day-by-Day Math Plans • ©The Mailbox® Books • TEC61392

Note to the teacher: Give the student seven different-colored crayons. Ask her to point to a flower and identify the number. Then have her color the flower a specific color.

Matching Sets to Numbers

Centers for the Week

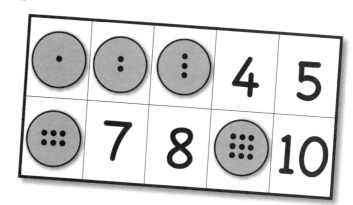

On a copy of page 159, label each box with a different number between 1 and 10. For each number, use a permanent marker to draw a corresponding dot set on a bottle (or milk) cap. A youngster chooses a cap, counts the dot set, and then places the cap atop the matching number.

Set out number cards 1 to 6 (cards on page 152–153). Get a jumbo die. A student rolls the die, counts the dots, and then finds the card with the matching number. He sets the card aside and continues in the same way.

Place number cards from 1 to 10 facedown. Provide a paper plate with a happy face and ten spring-style clothespins. A youngster flips a card, identifies the number, and clips the corresponding number of clothespins (hair) to the plate. She removes the clothespins, sets the card aside, and repeats the process.

2 3 4 5 6 7 8 9 10 1 2 3 4 5 6 7 8 9 10

	Group Time	Math Talk	
Monday	Set ten plastic eggs atop brown crinkle shreds (nest) and provide a sanitized foam egg carton. Display a number for students to identify. Then invite a child (farmer) to collect that many eggs and place them in the egg carton. Prompt the group to cluck their approval! ***Number identification, counting, forming sets***	Show number cards 4 and 8. Ask, "Which number matches the number of legs on a spider?" When the correct number is given, ask, "What else has eight legs?" Then ask, "Which number matches the number of legs on a cow?" and "What else has four legs?"	
Tuesday	Provide a poster board beehive and black pom-poms (bees). Place a number on the hive. Invite a child to identify the number and then "fly" that many bees to the hive. Prompt his classmates to say "buzz" as he maneuvers the bees. ***Number identification, counting, forming sets***	Write numbers 4, 5, and 6 on your board. Say, "Pretend you bought two new pairs of shoes. Which number matches the number of shoes you bought?" Then ask, "Which number represents three pairs of shoes?" Encourage youngsters to count their classmates' shoes to help them.	
Wednesday	Put different numbers of items in three plastic hoops and get a matching number card for each one. Give each number card to a different child. Set a timer and encourage each student to find the appropriate hoop and place her card in it before the timer goes off! ***Matching sets to numbers***	Set out number cards 2, 4 and 10. Ask, "Which number matches the number of wheels on a motorcycle?" When the correct number is given ask, "What else has two wheels?" Next ask, "Which number matches the number of wheels on a car?" Then ask, "What else has four wheels?"	
Thursday	Give each child cereal pieces (or another dry snack) and a mat like the one shown. Encourage him to identify each number and then place cereal pieces atop the corresponding dots. When he's finished, invite him to nibble the cereal! ***Number identification, counting, forming sets***	Write numbers "3" and "7" on your board. Say, "Pretend you ate three cherries and seven grapes. Which number shows the amount of cherries you ate and which shows the amount of grapes you ate?" Then ask, "What if you ate two more cherries? What number do we need to show how many cherries you ate?"	
Friday	Provide each child with a blue paper pond and ten yellow pom-poms (ducks). Gather number cards from 1 to 10. Display a card and lead students in saying, "I see [number] ducks, quack, quack, quack! Waddle in the pond to find a snack!" Then prompt students to "waddle" that many ducks onto their ponds. ***Number identification, counting, forming sets***	Pretend you build a road with ten blocks and a wall with eight blocks. Of these numbers (show number cards 5, 8, and 10), which one matches the number of blocks in the road? Which one matches the number of blocks in the wall? What is the remaining number? What could you do with five more blocks?	

Projects and More!

How Many Spots?
(See the directions on page 38.)

Gross-motor:
Help students form two lines in relay race fashion. Spread a duplicate set of number cards a distance from each team. Give each child a card programmed with a dot set to match one of the number cards. On your signal, the first child on each team runs to the cards, takes a number that matches his dot set, and then runs back. Play continues until all the cards are matched.

Simple Scenery
(See the directions on page 38.)

Practice pages: See pages 39 and 40 for practice with matching sets to numbers.

Cool Kite
(See the directions on page 38.)

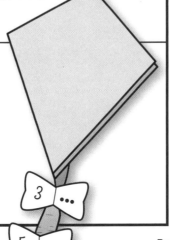

Bonus Ideas

Song: Give each child a copy of one number card from page 152 or 153. Display several items and then lead youngsters in the song shown. Help students count the items; then prompt each child to hold her card in the air if the number matches the number of items. Repeat with different numbers of items.

(tune: "The Muffin Man")

How many items in this set,
In this set, in this set?
How many items in this set?
Let's count them, and we'll see!

1 2 3 4 5 6 7 8 9 10

Take-home activity:
Place in a large resealable plastic bag a copy of the ten frame on page 159, ten number cards from 1 to 10, and ten pom-poms or craft foam shapes to place on the frame. Provide a note encouraging parents to practice matching sets to numbers with their child.

1 2 3 4 5 6 7 8 9 10

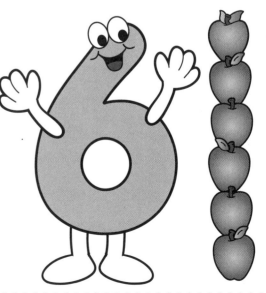

How Many Spots?

Materials for one project:

6" x 18" paper strip   black crayon
5 red ovals   glue
5 black semicircles

Steps:
1. Accordion-fold the strip to make six booklet pages; then title the first page of the booklet.
2. On each remaining page, glue an oval and a semicircle to make a ladybug. Draw legs and antennae on each ladybug.
3. Write a different number on each page and draw ladybug spots to correspond to that number.
4. If desired, use additional materials and repeat Steps 2 and 3 on the back of each page.

Simple Scenery

Draw a scene with a pond, tree trunks, and flower stems. Provide sets of cutouts that include fish, clouds, treetops, and flower tops. Provide glue sticks and number cards that correspond to the number of cutouts in each set. Divide the class into four groups. Each group takes a card, locates a set of cutouts with the corresponding number of items, and then glues the cutouts to the scene.

Cool Kite

Materials for one project:

tagboard kite   construction paper bows
crepe paper streamer   glue or tape

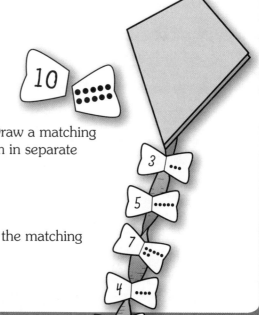

Setup: Write a different number on one half of each bow. Draw a matching dot set on the other half. Cut the bows in half and place them in separate piles.

Steps:
1. Attach the streamer to the kite.
2. Count the dot set on a bow half. Find the bow half with the matching number.
3. Align the bow halves and attach them to the streamer.
4. Repeat Steps 2 and 3 with the remaining bow halves.

Turtle's Toys

 Circle.

| 2 |  | |

| 8 | | |

| 5 | | |

| 10 | | |

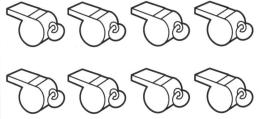

  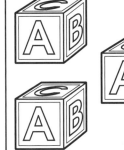 

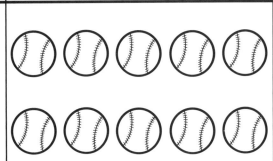 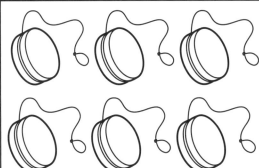

Note to the teacher: For each row, have a child name the number and then circle the matching set.

Fabulous Fruit!

 Cut.

Glue to match.

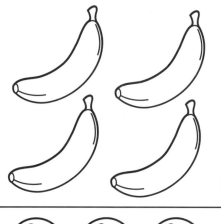

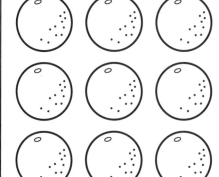

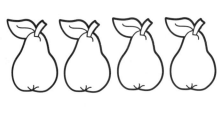

Day-by-Day Math Plans • ©The Mailbox® Books • TEC61392

9   7   5   4   10   3

Combining and Separating Sets

Centers for the Week

Provide a copy of page 156, dominoes, and ten counting chips (or counters from page 150). A student counts the dots on one side of a domino. He puts that many chips on one half of the mat and then repeats the process with the other side of the domino and mat. Then he counts all the chips on the mat to find the total number.

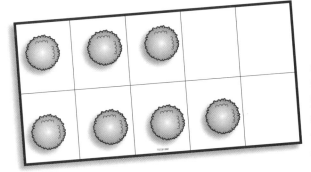

Set out a copy of page 159, ten pom-poms, and a bag containing number cards 1 to 5. A child takes a card and places that number of pom-poms in the top row of the frame. He puts the card back and repeats the process, placing the pom-poms in the bottom row. Then he counts the pom-poms in each row to find the total number.

Label dinosaur cutouts (pattern on page 45) with different numbers. Provide number cards (no higher than the lowest dinosaur number) and enough triangle cutouts (plates) to represent the highest number. A child takes a dinosaur, reads the number, and places that many plates on its back. Then he takes a number card, removes that many plates, and counts the number of plates that are left. He removes the plates and repeats the process.

	Group Time	**Math Talk**	
Monday	Set out a fishbowl cutout and ten fish cutouts. Put number cards 1 to 5 in a bag. Show a card for the group to identify. Invite a child to put that many fish in the bowl. Replace the card and repeat. Lead students in counting the total number of fish. ***Adding with objects***	Imagine you're playing with a friend. You have two toy cars, and he has two toy cars. How many cars do your friend and you have altogether? Pretend another friend who has two toy trucks joins you. How many vehicles are there now?	
Tuesday	Have each child put five to ten green pom-poms (frogs) on a brown paper log. Say, "[Number] frogs sat on a log basking in the sun. [Number] frogs jumped off the log to go have fun!" Have students hop that many frogs off the log and count how many are left. ***Subtracting with objects***	Pretend you have five carrot sticks. You give two of them to a friend. How many carrot sticks do you have left? If you eat two of those carrot sticks, how many would you have left?	
Wednesday	Draw a ten-rung ladder (launchpad) and attach it to a magnet board. Place on the first rung a tagboard rocket with magnetic tape attached. Label a spinner (page 149) 1 to 4. Have volunteers spin the spinner and move the rocket up. Lead students in saying each addition sentence. When the rocket reaches the top, lead the group in counting down to blastoff! ***Counting, saying addition sentences***	Imagine you see three bear cubs go into a cave. Then you see two cubs come out. How many bear cubs are left in the cave? Pretend Mama Bear goes into the cave. How many bears are in the cave now? Where do you think the two cubs that left the cave went?	
Thursday	Place up to ten felt shapes on your flannelboard. Have a child remove a certain number of shapes; then students count how many are left. Use felt accessories to model the subtraction sentence and lead students in reading the sentence. Repeat with a different number of shapes. ***Counting, reading subtraction sentences*** Ten minus four equals six!	Pretend you make ten snowballs. You toss four of them with your friend. How many snowballs do you have left? Pretend you make three more snowballs. How many do you have now? Your friend has to go home. What will you do with the snowballs?	
Friday	Add an addition sign to a blank number sentence (page 160) and place the sentence in a pocket chart. Ask up to five students (bunnies) to pretend to hop to a meadow. Put the corresponding number card in the sentence. Repeat. Help students count the total number of bunnies; then put the number card in the chart and lead students in reading the number sentence. ***Reading addition sentences***	Hold up four fingers on one hand. Hold up three fingers on your other hand. How many fingers are you holding up? Say the addition sentence.	

Projects and More!

Wandering Ducks

(See the directions on page 44.)

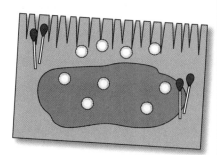

Partner Activity: Get a deck of playing cards. Evenly distribute all the number cards from 2 to 5. Give each student ten counters. In turn, each child sets out a card and then counts out the appropriate number of counters. Then the partners count the counters in each set to find the total number. They put the cards aside and continue.

Yummy Fries

(See the directions on page 44.)

Practice Page: See page 46 for practice with combining and separating sets.

Gross-motor: Arrange ten slightly weighted plastic bottles in bowling formation and provide a ball. Invite a small group of students to take turns bowling. After each child's turn, help her say the subtraction sentence according to the number of pins she knocks down. Then have her set the pins back up for the next player.

Bonus Ideas

Snack: Have a child place a number of thin banana slices on one half of a paper plate. Then instruct her to place a number of slices on the other half of the plate. Lead her in counting the slices together to find the total. Next, have her eat a certain number of slices and count again. Repeat until all the slices are eaten.

1 2 3 4 5 6 7 8 9 10

Song: Lead students in reciting this rhyme, holding up the appropriate numbers of fingers for each line. Repeat as desired, using different numbers.

[Five] little birdies sitting in a nest,
[Two] more came and joined the rest.
[Seven] little birdies singing a tune,
[Three] flew away
'Cause it was noon.
[Four] little birdies all alone,
A squirrel scampered by, and [two] were gone!
How many birdies are left?

1 2 3 4 5 6 7 8 9 10

Project Time

Wandering Ducks

Materials for one project:
blue pond-shaped cutout
green construction paper
cotton swabs
10 yellow pom-poms (ducks)
brown paint
glue
scissors

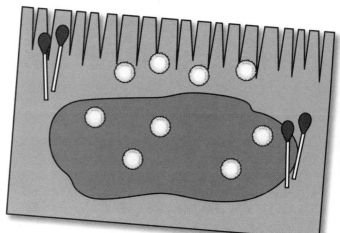

Setup: Cut the cotton swabs in half so they resemble cattails.

Steps:
1. Glue the pond cutout to the construction paper.
2. Fringe-cut the paper above the pond to make grass.
3. Roll the soft end of each cattail in the paint and then glue it to the project.
4. To use the project, place some ducks in the pond and the rest in the grass. Count the ducks in each group and then say a corresponding addition sentence. Repeat with a different combination of ducks.

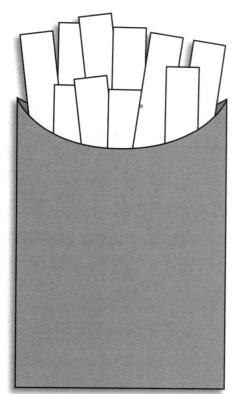

Yummy Fries

Materials for one project:
4½" x 12" tagboard
10 yellow tagboard strips (french fries)
scissors
glue

Steps:
1. Fold the tagboard and trim the ends as shown.
2. Glue the side edges together to make a french fry container.
3. Slide the french fries into the container.
4. To use the project, take some fries from the container and pretend to eat them. Count the number of fries left in the container. Say the corresponding subtraction sentence if desired. Replace the fries and repeat.

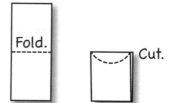

Fold. Cut.

TEC61392

Name _____

Crispy Carrots!

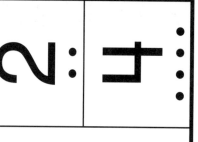

Add. Circle.

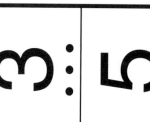

$$1 + 2 =$$

| 3 | : . . |
| 5 | : . . . . |

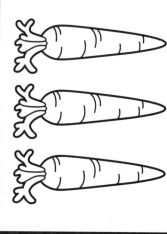

$$3 + 1 =$$

| 2 | : . |
| 4 | : . . . |

Subtract. Circle.

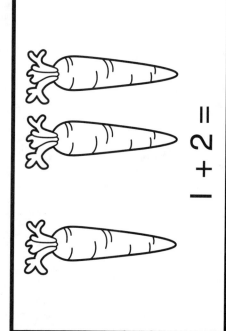

$$6 - 2 =$$

| 4 | : . . . |
| 5 | : . . . . |

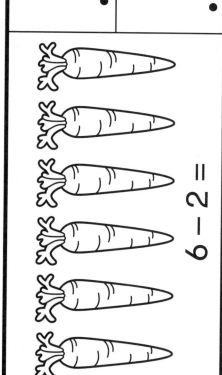

$$4 - 2 =$$

| 1 | . |
| 2 | : |

Day-by-Day Math Plans • ©The Mailbox® Books • TEC61392

Comparing Numbers

Centers for the Week

Label five craft foam bread shapes with numerals from 1 to 10. Repeat with a second set. Also number a set of craft foam cheese slices from 2 to 9. Spread out all the bread slices and place the cheese slices in a separate pile. A child takes a cheese slice and reads the number. She puts the cheese between two slices of bread: one with a higher number and one with a lower number than on the cheese. Then she puts the "sandwich" on a napkin and repeats the process.

Get a deck of playing cards. Evenly distribute between two students all the cards from two to ten. Have them stack the cards facedown. Each child flips a card. The student with the higher number keeps both flipped cards. If the cards show the same number, each child flips another card. Play continues until all the cards are flipped. As an alternative, players keep the cards when the lower number is flipped.

Label a large sheet of paper as shown. Get a top hat (or make one from an oatmeal container) and a craft stick (wand). Place number cards 1 to 4 and 6 to 10 in the hat. A child waves the wand above the hat and says, "Abracadabra!" Then he picks a card and places it on the appropriate side of the mat saying, "Ta da!" Then he hands the wand to the next player. Play continues until the hat is empty.

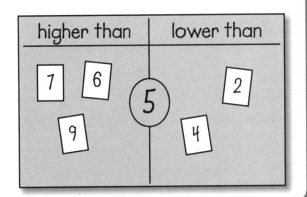

2 3 4 5 6 7 8 9 10 1 2 3 4 5 6 7 8 9 10

	Group Time	Math Talk
Monday	Spread faceup on the floor ten banana cutouts labeled with numbers 1 to 10. Display a number card for students to identify. Invite a volunteer to find a banana labeled with a number less than the number on the card. If he's correct, youngsters mimic a monkey. If not, they stay still. Continue in the same way. **Less than**	Imagine you have one friend who lives at 10 Maple Road and another who lives at 7 Maple Road. Which address number is greater? Name an address number that is less than 7 Maple Road.
Tuesday	Divide the class in two. Ask one group to clap five times. Write the number on chart paper. Have the other group clap three times. Record the number and then ask students which group clapped a greater number of times. Circle the appropriate number. Repeat with other actions. **Greater than**	Pretend you're at a soccer game. One player is wearing a shirt labeled with "6." Another player is wearing a shirt labeled with "9." Which number is less, six or nine? What number is one greater than nine?
Wednesday	Label shirt cutouts with numbers 1 to 10. Hang the "5" shirt on a clothesline. Invite a child to choose a shirt. Ask students whether the number is less than or greater than the number five. Then help the child hang the shirt on the appropriate side of the shirt labeled "5". Continue in the same way. **Less than, greater than**	Let's say you buy two birthday cards. Each card has a "6" on it to represent a child's age. Would the number on one card be greater than, less than, or equal to the number on the other card? Name a number greater than six and less than eight.
Thursday	Give each child a spring-style clothespin and a tagboard strip labeled with numbers 1 to 10. Hold up a number card and ask students to clip the clothespin on the strip to a number that is less than, greater than, or equal to yours. **Less than, greater than, equal to**	Imagine you're playing a game of ring toss. You toss one ring onto a cone labeled "8" and another ring onto a cone labeled "7." Which cone has the greater number? You toss one more ring onto a cone labeled "5." Is five greater than or less than seven?
Friday	Place chairs in a circle. Put a number card under each chair. Play music as children walk around the chairs. Stop the music and have each child sit in a chair and remove the card. Show a number. Ask each student to hold up her card if her number is greater than yours. Play several rounds, having students hold up cards to reflect numbers less than and equal to your number. **Greater than, less than, equal to**	Pretend you buy two raffle tickets. The number on one ticket is "5." The number on the other ticket is "3." Which number is less than the other? 

Vroom!
(See the directions on page 50.)

The first car's number is greater than
The second car in the pack,
But there's a number less than theirs
On the car that's in the back!

Gross-motor: Place number cards from 1 to 10 in a bag. Pull out a card for students to identify. Repeat with a second card. If the second number is greater than the first number, youngsters stomp their feet. If it is less than the first number, they tiptoe in place. Return the cards to the bag and repeat the activity.

Greater Than, Less Than
(See the directions on page 50.)

Practice page: See page 52 for practice with comparing numbers.

Partner activity: Give each child (baker) a baking tray and ten craft foam cookies. Spread number cards from 1 to 10 facedown. Have each baker take a card and place a corresponding number of cookies on her tray. After the bakers model their numbers, have them compare the batches of cookies to see who has the greater number.

Time filler: Write a number from 1 to 10 on a dry-erase board. Have students identify the number; then ask them to name numbers that are less than (or greater than) that number. Write the numbers on the board and review them with the group. Wipe the board clean and repeat with a different number.

1 2 3 4 5 6 7 8 9 10

Transition: Display a number card and have a child identify it. Display a second card and have her tell whether that number is greater than, less than, or equal to the number on the first card. After confirming a correct answer, have her move to the next activity.

1 2 3 4 5 6 7 8 9 10

Vroom!

Materials for one project:

construction paper
3 car cutouts (patterns on page 51)
marker
glue

Setup: Write the poem shown on a paper rectangle with a decorative edge.

The first car's number is greater than
The second car in the pack,
But there's a number less than theirs
On the car that's in the back!

Steps:

1. Glue the cars to the construction paper as shown.
2. Write a number on the second car.
3. On the first car, write a number greater than the number on the second car.
4. On the third car, write a number less than the number on the second car.
5. Glue the poem to the page. (If desired, glue the pages between two covers to make a class book.)

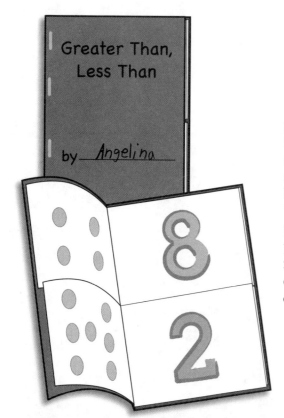

Greater Than, Less Than

With this unique booklet, youngsters flip the pages for a different number comparison each time! To prepare a booklet for each child, fold two sheets of copy paper in half; then add one more half sheet to make five booklet pages. Staple the pages between a folded construction paper cover labeled "Greater Than, Less Than." Then cut the copy paper in half to make five top pages and five bottom pages. Help a child write, trace, or stamp a different number from 1 to 10 on each page, and then put a corresponding number of sticky dots on the back of each page.

TEC61392

TEC61392

TEC61392

Name _____

Up, Up, and Away!

Listen and do.

1

3   6   2

7   4   8

10

Note to the teacher: Have a child study the hot-air balloon. Ask her to find the numbers less than 5 on the hot-air balloon and color the spaces blue. Next, ask her to find the numbers greater than 5 and color the spaces red. Then have her find a number less than 2 and color the space yellow.

52

g Numbers

___ for the Week

Place rice in your sensory table (or in a large plastic tub). Gather assorted number cards from 11 to 20 and hide them in the rice. Place a number line nearby. A student finds a number and says its name. Then she places the number card below its match on the number line. She continues with each number card in the sensory table.

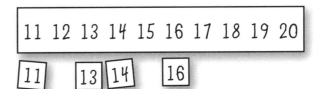

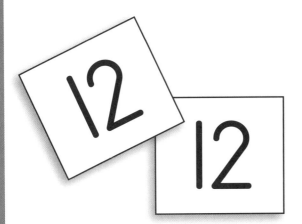

For this partner game, cut out two sets of assorted number cards from copies of pages 152–155. Put one set in a bag and spread the remaining set faceup. One child takes a card from the bag. He names the number, keeping it concealed from his partner. The partner finds the matching number; then the pair compares the two cards to confirm that they match. The partners switch tasks and continue taking turns until the bag is empty.

Program a sheet of blank chart paper with desired numbers from 11 to 20 as shown. Provide store flyers, scissors, and glue. A youngster selects a number on the chart and names it. Then she looks for the corresponding number in a flyer. When she finds the number, she cuts it out and glues it to the appropriate section of the chart. She continues in the same way.

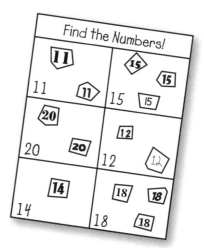

	Group Time	**Math Talk**
Monday	Gather assorted number cards including 2, 10, 16, and 18. Display the cards, in turn, for students to identify. After naming the number 2, say, "Stomp your shoe!" After 10, say, "Squawk like a hen!" After 16, say, "Jump on a trampoline!" After 18 say, "Can you look mean?" *Identifying numbers, following directions*	Picture a number line from one to ten. Count backward from ten and stop at the number four. If you count backward two more numbers, what number is it? *Ten, nine, eight,…*
Tuesday	Label half of a class supply of large flower cutouts with assorted numbers from 11 to 20. Scatter the flowers on the floor. Invite your little bees to buzz around the flowers. Ring a bell and prompt two bees to land on each flower. Have each pair identify the number; then begin again. *Identifying numbers, gross-motor*	Pretend you pick a number card that has a one and a zero. What two-digit number do the numbers represent? If you pick a card with a two and a zero, what two-digit number is that?
Wednesday	Place assorted number cards in a pocket chart. Place a duplicate set of cards in a bag. Seat students in a circle. Play music as children pass the bag around the circle. Stop the music and have the child with the bag pull a number for the group to identify. Have her put the card in the chart with the matching number; then restart the music. *Identifying and matching numbers*	Picture a number line from ten to 20. Name the number that comes right before the number 11. What number comes right after number 15? Name a number and then tell the number that comes next.
Thursday	Gather number cards from 11 to 20. Display a card and have students identify the number. Then announce a direction that corresponds to the number, such as "Touch your toes [twelve] times" or "Clap your hands [fifteen] times." *Identifying numbers, following directions*	Imagine you're looking at a calendar. What number comes between the numbers 12 and 14? What number comes between 11 and 13? Name two numbers and then tell the number that comes between them.
Friday	Arrange number cards from 11 to 20 in numerical order. Randomly place an identical set of cards facedown. Have students identify the first number in the row; then invite a child to flip a card. If the card shows an 11, she places it below the matching card. If not, she turns the card back over. Repeat until all the cards are faceup and in numerical order. *Identifying numbers, number order*	Pretend you lay down number cards from one to 12. Then you lay down the next two cards. What numbers are on those cards?

Projects and More!

Numerical Cookies

(See the directions on page 56.)

Gross-motor: Make several large number cards. Mark a line for youngsters to stand behind. Stand a distance from students. Display a card and have youngsters identify the number; then prompt them to take that many giant steps toward you. Continue with other numbers and gross-motor movements until everyone reaches you.

Nifty Number Display

(See the directions on page 56.)

Practice pages: See pages 57 and 58 for practice naming numbers.

Number Bug

(See the directions on page 56.)

Bonus Ideas

Transition: Attach laminated number cards from 1 to 20 to the floor near the classroom door. When it's time to line up, call each child to stand on a designated number.

11 12 13 14 15 16 17 18 19 20

Song: Give each child a number card. Then lead students in singing the song shown, prompting each child to hold his card in the air when his number is named.

(tune: "If You're Happy and You Know It")

If you have a number [12] hold it up!
If you have a number [12] hold it up!
Show your number [12] to me.
Hold it up for all to see.
If you have a number [12] hold it up!

11 12 13 14 15 16 17 18 19 20

Project Time

Numerical Cookies

This fun activity combines baking with number identification! Roll out tubes of prepared sugar cookie dough. Have each child use number-shaped cookie cutters to cut a number from the dough. As she works, encourage her to chant, "Homemade cookies are good to eat! Number [number] will be my treat!" Bake the cookies and then invite youngsters to eat their homemade snack.

Nifty Number Display

This project creates a functional display! Give each child a sheet of tagboard labeled with a different number from 1 to 20. Provide markers, stickers, rubber stamps, and stamp pads. Invite him to decorate the number using desired materials. Then mount the projects with the title "Nifty Numbers, We've Got Plenty! Name Them Now From 1 to 20!" Use the board to reinforce number recognition and identification skills.

Number Bug

Materials for one project:

4 jumbo craft sticks   five 3" lengths of pipe cleaner
permanent marker   masking tape

Steps:
1. Draw a face on one end of a craft stick; then write the numbers 1 to 5 as shown.
2. Label each remaining stick with numbers 6 to 10, 11 to 15, and 16 to 20.
3. Bend each pipe cleaner piece in half; then tape one above the face (antennae) and one to the bottom of each stick (legs).
4. Place the sticks in numerical order. Then flip the sticks facedown and use masking tape to connect them.

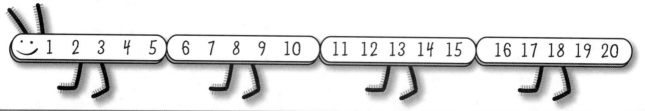

Name _____

Listen and do.

Ocean View

5

8

11

13

12

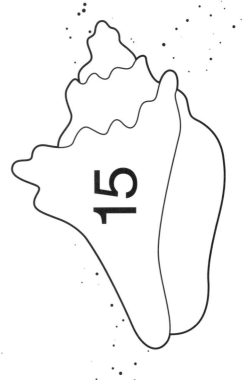

15

Day-by-Day Math Plans • ©The Mailbox® Books • TEC61392

Note to the teacher: Ask a child to point to a specific object on a copy of the page. Help her identify the number and then have her color that item. Continue in the same way.

Pretty Planter

Connect the dots from 1 to 20.
Name each number as you work.

18   19   20   1   2   3

17 16   5   4

15   6

14   7

13   8

12   11   10   9

Day-by-Day Math Plans • ©The Mailbox® Books • TEC61392

Matching Sets to Numbers

Centers for the Week

Lightly attach to each of several tagboard peacock bodies (pattern on page 63) a number card from 11 to 20. Provide colorful spring-style clothespins (feathers). A youngster takes a peacock, reads the number, and then clips a matching number of feathers to the body. For additional practice, simply replace the numbers on each peacock.

Label ten paper plates with numbers 11 to 20. For each plate, draw a matching set of blue dots (blueberries) on a tan craft foam pancake. Provide a spatula. A child counts the blueberries on a pancake. Then he uses the spatula to put the pancake on a plate with the matching number. He continues until each pancake is on the appropriate plate.

Provide a red tagboard pizza (no toppings), red plastic chips or milk caps (pepperoni), and several number cards from 11 to 20 (cards on pages 153–155). A student takes a card and puts the corresponding number of pepperoni slices on the pizza. Then he pretends to cut a slice and eat it. He removes the pepperoni and repeats the process. For added fun, put the pizza on a pizza pan and provide a plastic pizza cutter.

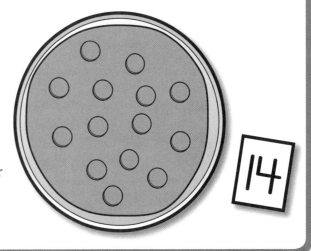

Group Time	Math Talk
Monday Spread number cards from 11 to 20 facedown. Invite a child (exercise trainer) to name an exercise for the group to perform. Then have her flip a card and tell how many repetitions in the set. Prompt students to count aloud as they exercise. **Matching sets to numbers, gross-motor**  *Eleven jumping jacks!*	Pretend you bake 12 cupcakes and 20 cookies. Looking at these two number cards (display the appropriate cards), which one matches the number of cupcakes and which one matches the number of cookies? What if you ate two cupcakes? What number would you need to show how many cupcakes are left?
Tuesday Put a tree cutout on the floor and number cards in a bag. Provide orange pom-poms (oranges). Lead the group in chanting, "Orange tree, orange tree, oh so bare! How many oranges should be there?" Ask a child to take a card from the bag and identify the number. Then have him place that many oranges on the tree. Continue in the same way. ***Identifying numbers, matching sets to numbers***	Imagine you have 13 pennies in your piggy bank. Of these two slips of paper (show two paper scraps labeled "13" and "19"), which would you tuck into your bank as a reminder of how many pennies you have? How many more pennies would you need to use the paper labeled "19"?
Wednesday For this small-group activity, put in separate resealable plastic bags items in sets of 11 to 20. Provide the corresponding number cards. Spill the items from a bag and lead students in counting them. Replace the items and have a child place the bag near the matching card. Repeat. ***Counting, matching sets to numbers***	Pretend you have 14 seashells in your pail. Of these two tags (show two tags marked "14" and "18"), which would you attach to your pail to show the number of shells? What if you collected four more shells? Could you use the tag labeled "18"? How do you know?
Thursday Gather pom-poms, craft sticks, and crayons. Give each child one item. Name an item and then prompt youngsters with that item to place them in a group on the floor. Lead students in counting the items and then invite a volunteer to choose a matching number card from several you present. Repeat with the remaining items. ***Matching sets to numbers***	Imagine you go to the farmers' market. You buy ten red apples and six green apples. Which of these bags (show two bags labeled "10" and "6") would you put the red apples in? Is the other bag labeled with an appropriate number for the green apples? What if the bag for the green apples were labeled with an "8"? What would you do?
Friday Distribute a class supply of cards labeled with numbers from 11 to 20. Draw a set of circles on a dry-erase board and then lead students in counting the circles. Prompt youngsters who have the matching number to display their cards. Repeat the process. ***Matching sets to numbers***	Pretend you put 11 big marbles in one container and 15 small marbles in another container. Which of these labels (show two labels marked "11" and "15") would you attach to the container of big marbles and which would you attach to the container of small marbles? What if you lost one of the big marbles? What number would need to be on the label?

Projects and More!

Buzz...
(See the directions on page 62.)

Snack:
Provide each child with a cup of cookie-style cereal and a paper plate labeled with a number from 11 to 20. Help her identify the number on her plate. Then encourage her to place a matching number of cereal pieces on her plate. Check for accuracy and then invite her to eat the cereal and any leftovers in the cup!

Busy Builders
(See the directions on page 62.)

Practice page:
See page 64 for practice with matching sets to numbers.

How Many Sprinkles?
(See the directions on page 62.)

Bonus Ideas

Transition:
Give each child a card programmed with a dot set from 11 to 20. Before lining up, ask each child to quietly count the dots in his set. Then display a number card and prompt each student with a dot set that matches the number to line up. Continue in the same way.

11 12 13 14 15 16 17 18 19 20

Time filler:
Display a number from 11 to 20. Ask students to identify the number and then invite a volunteer to tell a way to act out the number. For example, he may choose to clap, stomp, touch his toes, or pat his knees. Then have him lead his classmates in the counting fun!

11 12 13 14 15 16 17 18 19 20

Project Time

Buzz...

What's the buzz about? Numbers and sets! Give each child a beehive cutout labeled with a number from 11 to 20. Encourage him to make a matching number of yellow fingerprints on the hive. Then invite him to use a fine-tip black marker to add bee details to each print. Display the projects with the title "Buzzing About Numbers and Sets!"

11 in a set.

This is what you get!

Busy Builders

Have pairs of children collaborate to make this class book! Give a pair of students between 11 and 20 blocks. Snap a photo of the pair with the scattered blocks; then encourage them to build a structure. Snap a photo of the structure; then mount the two photos on paper programmed with text similar to that shown. Bind the pages between two covers and title the book "What Do You Get With a Set?"

How Many Sprinkles?

Give each child an ice cream scoop cutout and a tagboard cone labeled with a number from 11 to 20. Provide mini pom-poms (sprinkles) and glue. Have a child glue the ice cream scoop to the cone. Help her identify the number on the cone; then encourage her to glue that many sprinkles to the scoop.

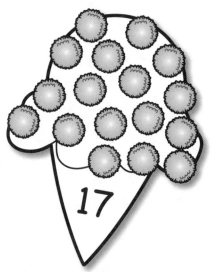

TEC61392

Name _____

Spectacular Sprinkles!

Cut.

Glue to match.

Day-by-Day Math Plans • ©The Mailbox® Books • TEC61392

| 11 | 8 | 20 | 17 | 15 | 10 |

Combining and Separating Sets

Centers for the Week

For this partner center, provide rolling pins, cookie cutters, a large cookie sheet, and play dough in two colors. Each partner chooses a dough color. Then she rolls out her dough and uses a cookie cutter to cut out five to ten cookies. Each child counts her cookies as she places them on the tray; then the pair counts all the cookies to determine the total number.

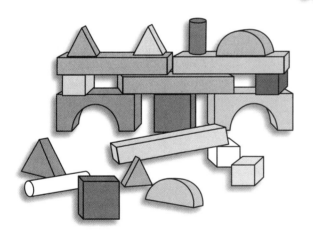

Provide a set of 20 assorted building blocks. A youngster uses the blocks to build a structure. He counts the number of blocks used and then gently pushes the structure to knock it over. Then he counts the number of blocks left standing.

Make a simple forest mat. Collect two sets of ten bear manipulatives, each set in a different color. Put the sets in separate bags. A student takes a handful of bears from a bag. Then she counts each bear as she helps it meander into the forest. She repeats the process with the other bag. Then she counts the total number of bears in the forest.

Group Time	Math Talk

Monday

Use masking tape to divide a blanket (flying carpet) in half; then spread it on the floor. Invite five or more children to sit on one side of the blanket. Repeat with the other side. Lead students in counting each group, and then the total number of youngsters combined. Then take an imaginary carpet ride! ***Counting, addition***

Imagine you pull ten carrots from your garden. A bunny comes along and eats three of them. How many carrots do you have left? Another bunny comes along and eats two more carrots. How many carrots are left now? What should you do with the rest of the carrots?

Tuesday

Put a felt tree on a flannelboard and up to 20 apples on the tree. Lead the group in counting the apples. Then say, for example, "Twelve apples in a tree. Two fell. How many are left? Let's count and see!" Remove two apples. Lead students in counting the remaining apples. Repeat with different numbers of apples. ***Counting, subtraction***

Pretend you want to play a game of marbles. You need 12 marbles but have only six. How many more marbles do you need? If you have the 12 marbles and lose two of them, how many will you have left? What could you do to keep from losing the marbles?

Wednesday

Scatter 20 pom-poms (gumballs) on a gumball machine drawing. Have a child roll a die, count the dots, and remove that many gumballs. Lead the group in counting the remaining gumballs and then in saying the subtraction sentence. Repeat the process until no gumballs are left. ***Counting, saying subtraction sentences***

Let's say you're on a picnic. You walk away from the blanket, leaving 13 cookies on a plate. A squirrel scampers by and snatches three cookies. How many cookies are left? What might you learn from this experience?

Thursday

Set out two trays. Give each child a cotton ball. Have several students put their cotton balls in one tray. Have a few other children put their cotton balls in the other tray. Lead youngsters in counting the total number of cotton balls and then saying the addition sentence. Return the cotton balls and repeat. ***Counting, saying addition sentences***

Pretend your family is having a yard sale. You post five yard sale signs, and your grandma posts five. How many signs are posted in all? The wind blows and knocks down two signs. How many signs are posted now? What could you do?

Friday

Write the total number of students on a laminated number sentence (see page 160). Count the students with brown hair and write the number. Count the remaining students, write the number, and then lead youngsters in reading the subtraction sentence. Wipe off the sentence and repeat with other characteristics. ***Counting, reading subtraction sentences***

$$18 - 8 = 10$$

Imagine you go outside after a rainstorm and see seven worms in one mud puddle and six in another. How many worms do you see altogether? All of a sudden, two more worms wiggle into the puddle! How many worms are there now? What could you do with the worms?

Projects and More!

Jazzy Jewelry

(See the directions on page 68.)

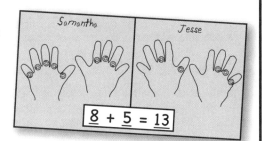

Samantha   Jesse

$$\underline{8} + \underline{5} = \underline{13}$$

Snack: Give each child 20 fish-shaped crackers on a blue napkin or paper. Announce a certain number of fish for students to "catch" and eat. Then have youngsters count the remaining fish. Repeat the process until all the fish are eaten.

Crafty Counter

(See the directions on page 68.)

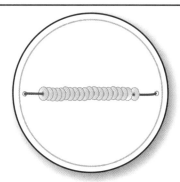

Practice pages: See pages 69 and 70 for practice matching sets to numbers.

Gross-motor: Have youngsters stand in an area opposite your group-time area. Count the number of children aloud. Call on several youngsters to skip to the group area and sit. Lead students in saying the subtraction sentence. Then have the students rejoin the group. Repeat the activity with different youngsters and gross-motor movements.

Bonus Ideas

Time filler: Practice a bit of addition when you have a few minutes to spare! Give each student a paper strip programmed with his first and last name. Have him count the letters in his first name and then count the letters in his last name. Then have him count the total number of letters.

11 12 13 14 15 16 17 18 19 20

Rhyme: Lead students in this fun fingerplay to practice simple subtraction! Then replace the number in the second line to repeat the activity.

Show all your fingers, one to ten.
Now, put [three] fingers down.
Count the fingers that you see.
How many are left? What can it be?

11 12 13 14 15 16 17 18 19 20

Jazzy Jewelry

For this partner project, divide a large sheet of construction paper as shown. Provide large sequins and glue. Help each child trace her hands on a side of the page and then write her name. Instruct her to glue up to ten sequins (rings) on her finger tracings as shown. Then help the pair write the addition equation on a blank number sentence (see page 160) and attach it to the page.

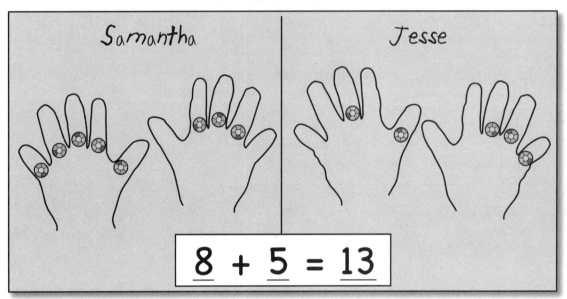

Crafty Counter

Materials for one project:

heavyweight paper plate
20 O-shaped cereal pieces
thin twine
hole-puncher
tape

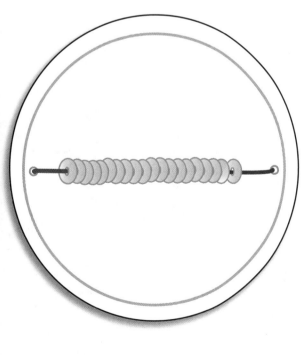

Steps:

1. Punch a hole in opposite sides of the plate as shown.
2. Thread a length of twine through one hole; then string the cereal onto the twine.
3. Thread the loose end of the twine through the remaining hole. Pull the twine taut (but not too tight) and tie the ends together.
4. Tape the twine to the back of the plate to secure it in place. Then use this simple abacus to practice separating and combining the cereal pieces.

Name _____

More Cookies, Please!

 Cut.

Add.

 Glue.

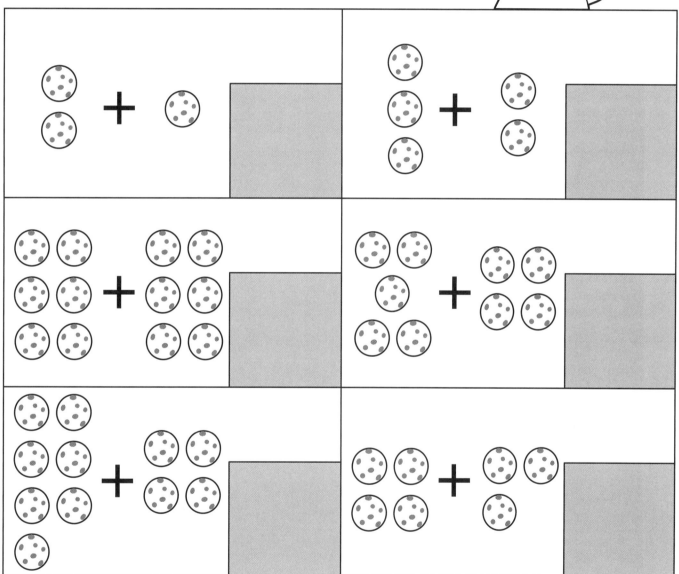

Day-by-Day Math Plans • ©The Mailbox® Books • TEC61392

5

12

3

9

11

7

Name _____

Busy Bees

Subtract.

 Cross out the 🐝 to help you.

7 – 3 = _____

10 – 4 = _____

12 – 5 = _____

11 – 6 = _____

14 – 6 = _____

17 – 7 = _____

13 – 4 = _____

20 – 8 = _____

Tens and Ones

Centers for the Week

Put 11 to 19 seashells in a tub of sand. Label a sand pail with the number "10" and place it nearby. A child counts out ten shells and places them in the pail. He counts the number of leftovers in the tub. Then he says, "There is one group of ten shells and [number] shells left in the sand." Change the number of shells in the tub each day to keep interest high.

Provide a collection of 19 spider rings. A child gathers a set of more than ten rings. Then she puts one ring on each finger. She counts the rings on her fingers and then counts the leftover rings in her set. Then she says, "I have ten spider rings on my fingers and [number] rings left over." She repeats the activity with a different set of more than ten.

Set out 19 pieces of bowtie pasta (butterflies) and a copy of page 75. A child puts ten butterflies on the bush and several other butterflies in the sky. She says, "There is a group of ten butterflies on the bush and [number] butterflies in the sky!" Then she removes the butterflies from the mat and repeats the activity, placing a different number of butterflies in the sky.

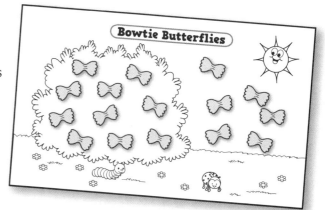

Bowtie Butterflies

	Group Time	Math Talk	

Monday

Set out a leaf cutout and 16 red pom-poms (ladybugs). Have students count aloud as you place ten ladybugs on the leaf. Then help youngsters count the leftover ladybugs. Write the equation "10 + 6 = 16." Repeat the activity with different amounts of ladybugs from 11 to 19. **Composing numbers**

Let's say you have 11 rings in your jewelry box. Do you have enough to put one ring on each of your ten fingers? Will there be any rings left? Explain. What will you do with the extra ring?

Tuesday

Draw a parking lot with ten spaces. Provide 11 to 19 vehicles. Ask a child to park one vehicle in each space as her classmates count aloud. Lead students in counting the vehicles still waiting. Then write the equation "10 + [number] = [number]." Repeat the activity with different numbers of cars. **Composing numbers**

Imagine you have 13 fish in a fishbowl. Do you have enough to put ten fish in a separate fishbowl? How many fish will be left in the original bowl? Why would you put ten fish in a separate bowl?

Wednesday

Provide a play dough cake and 11 to 19 birthday candles. Have youngsters count as you put ten candles on the cake. Then help students count the leftover candles. Write the equation "10 + [number] = [number]" and lead children in a round of a birthday song. Repeat the activity with different numbers. **Composing numbers**

Pretend you count 15 birds on the ground. Ten of the birds fly up into a tree. How many birds are left on the ground? How do you know?

Thursday

Scatter 11 to 19 die-cut fish on a paper pond. Help students count the fish. Say, "Is there enough fish to catch a group of ten? Do you think there will be any fish left?" Then have a volunteer help you "catch" ten fish. Help youngsters count the leftover fish. Then write the equation "[number] = 10 + [number]." **Decomposing numbers**

Imagine you catch 12 tadpoles in a net. You try to dump the tadpoles into a pail, but only ten go in. How many tadpoles are left in the net? What would you do with the extra tadpoles?

Friday

Lead students in counting 15 black mini pom-poms (ants) as you place them on a paper anthill. Say, "Ten ants leave to search for food." Move ten ants off the hill. Help students count the ants left on the anthill; then write the equation "15 = 10 + [number]." For added fun, have children wiggle like they have ants in their pants! **Decomposing numbers**

Pretend you're filling goody bags, and each bag gets ten pieces of candy. You have 16 pieces of candy left. Do you have enough candy to fill one more goody bag? How about two bags? Explain.

Projects and More!

Buggy for Tens and Ones!

(See the directions on page 74.)

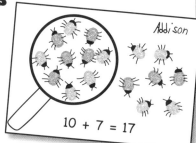

Snack: Give each child a plastic cup and a napkin with 13 snack crackers. Ask each child to count out ten crackers and place them in his cup. Have him count the leftover crackers on the napkin and then help him say a corresponding equation.

Wonderful Worms

(See the directions on page 74.)

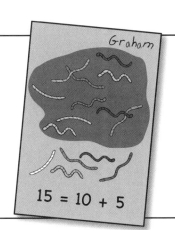

> **Practice page:** See page 76 for practice with tens and ones.

Partner activity: Provide 19 craft sticks and a disposable cup. One child counts out ten craft sticks and puts them in the cup. The other child counts out between one and nine of the remaining sticks and places them near the cup. Then the youngsters say a corresponding equation. The partners switch tasks and repeat the process.

Bonus Ideas

Song: Lead students in singing this simple song to help them remember the concept of a group of ten!

A Group of Ten
(tune: "The Farmer in the Dell")

When you count out ten things,
When you count out ten things,
Treat those things as a group.
You've made a group of ten!

11 12 13 14 15 16 17 18 19 20

Take-home activity: For each child, send a note home in a large, resealable plastic bag asking parents to help their child gather 11 to 19 items. At school, have each child count out ten of his items and the leftovers. Help him say a corresponding equation. Have students switch bags and repeat the activity.

11 12 13 14 15 16 17 18 19 20

Project Time

Buggy for Tens and Ones!

Provide a circle tracer, a stamp pad, and a fine-tip marker. Have each child trace a circle onto one side of a sheet of paper and then draw a handle on the circle so it resembles a magnifying glass. Instruct her to use the stamp pad to make ten fingerprints inside the circle; then have her draw insect details on each print. Encourage her to make one to nine more insects beside the magnifying glass. Then help her write a corresponding equation on the page. Bind the pages between two covers to make a class book titled "Buggy for Ten and Ones!"

Wonderful Worms

Materials for one project:
12" x 18" green construction paper
brown puddle cutout
yarn
glue
marker

Setup: Cut between 11 and 19 lengths of yarn (worms).

Steps:
1. Glue the puddle to the paper.
2. Count the worms and then glue ten of them to the puddle.
3. Glue the remaining worms to the "grass" beside the puddle.
4. Write "[number] = 10 + [number]."

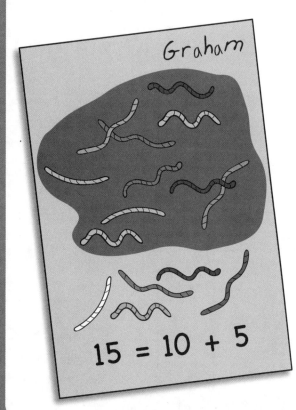

Bowtie Butterflies

Day-by-Day Math Plans • ©The Mailbox® Books • TEC61392

Note to the teacher: Use with the third center activity on page 71.

Insect Inspection

 Cut. Count. Glue.

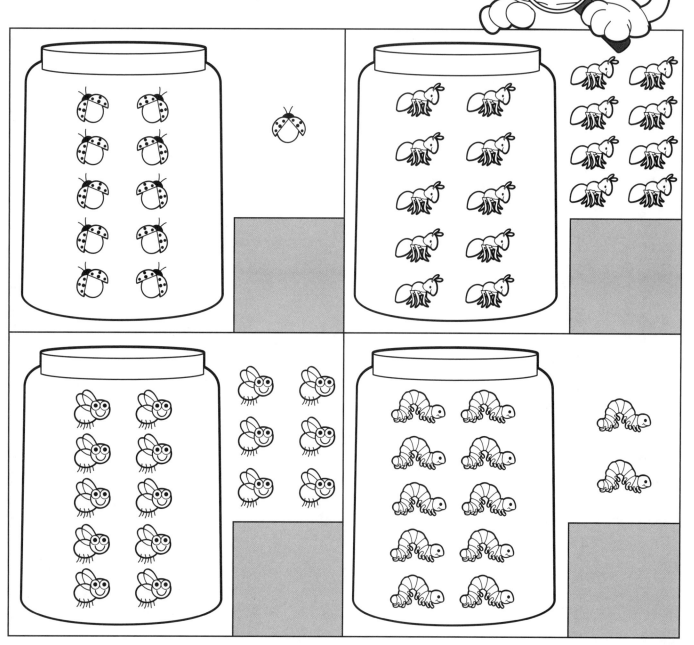

| 16 | 12 | 11 | 18 |

Basic Shapes

Centers for the Week

Cut squares and circles from craft foam and float them in your water table. Label one container with a circle and one with a square. A youngster uses tongs to remove a shape from the water. Then he identifies it and places it in the correct container.

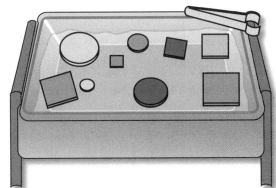

Provide play dough and straws in different lengths. If desired, provide shape cutouts as references. Encourage youngsters to build shapes by connecting straws with small balls of play dough.

Draw triangles in different orientations on large index cards. Also make several distracter shape cards. Place the stack of cards facedown near a tray of sand (or rice). Two students visit the center, and one child chooses a card. The students decide whether the card shows a triangle. If it does, the youngster who pulled the card uses an unsharpened pencil to draw the shape in the sand. Students repeat the process, taking turns, for each remaining card.

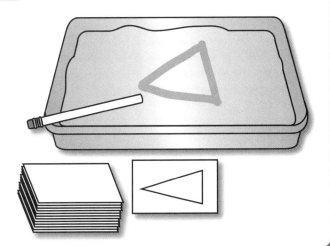

	Group Time	**Math Talk**
Monday	Place felt shapes on your flannelboard. Say, "Pick out triangles, 1, 2, 3! Show those triangles to me!" Then have a child remove all the triangles from the flannelboard. Replace the shapes. Then repeat the activity, naming a different shape in the chant. ***Recognizing shapes***	What shape is the door? Why do you think doors are this shape? Do you think a different shape would work well for a door? Why or why not?
Tuesday	Arrange chairs in a circle, facing outward, and tape a shape cutout to each chair. Play music as students walk around the circle. Stop the music and have each child sit in a chair. Prompt him to identify the shape on his chair. Continue for several rounds. ***Identifying shapes***	What shape is a pizza? Let's pretend we can only put toppings on the pizza that are circles. What could we use as toppings?
Wednesday	Place shape cutouts in a bag and seat students in a circle. Play music and have students pass the bag around the circle. Stop the music and prompt a child to take a shape from the bag and identify it. Have him replace the shape before playing another round. ***Identifying shapes***	Let's pretend that no one is allowed to have anything that is a circle. What types of things would we have to do without?
Thursday	Place a piece of bulletin board paper on the floor. Tell students that you are a baker and you're going to make a batch of cookies. Say, "The first cookie I want to make is a yellow circle." Have a child choose a yellow crayon and make a yellow circle on the paper. Continue with other colorful cookie shapes. ***Forming shapes***	What is your favorite shape? Why is it your favorite?
Friday	Read aloud *Mouse Shapes* by Ellen Stoll Walsh. Then encourage youngsters to glue together shape cutouts to make crafty mice—just like the big scary mice the mouse characters make in the story! ***Responding to a story***	Can you make a circle with your fingers? How about a triangle, square, or rectangle? Which shape was the easiest to make? Which one was most difficult?

Mouse Shapes
Ellen Stoll Walsh
Creator of Mouse Paint and Mouse Count

Projects and More!

Thinking About Shapes

(See the directions on page 80.)

Gross motor: Attach masking tape shapes to the floor. Play a musical recording and have students dance around the shapes. Then stop the music and name one of the shapes. Encourage youngsters to quickly place one foot on the named shape. Continue for several rounds.

Shape Booklet Collage

(See the directions on page 80.)

Practice page: See pages 81 and 82 for practice with basic shapes.

Cheese, Please!

(See the directions on page 80.)

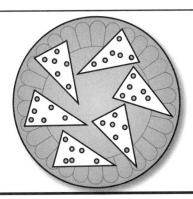

Bonus Ideas

Transition: Give each child a small shape cutout (ticket). Call on a youngster to line up, encouraging him to give you his ticket and name the shape. Continue with each remaining child until you've collected all the tickets and students are ready to travel down the hall.

Song: Hide circle cutouts around your room. Then lead students in singing the song shown and encourage them to hunt for the circles.

(sung to the tune of "This Old Man")

Circles here, circles there,
Circles, circles everywhere!
Let's all look for circles.
Where could they all be?
Let's all look, and we shall see!

Project Time

Thinking About Shapes

What's on your youngsters' minds? Shapes! To prepare, take a head-and-shoulders photo of each child looking thoughtful. Help her trim around the photo and attach it to a sheet of construction paper. Then have her draw a thought bubble above her head and draw colorful shapes in the bubble.

Shape Booklet Collage

This shapely project combines a booklet with collage! Gather a variety of materials such as magazines, tissue paper, construction paper scraps, and scrapbook paper. Make a simple, blank four-page booklet for each child. Encourage him to write (or dictate) the name of a different shape on each page. Then have him cut shapes from the materials and glue them on the appropriate pages.

Cheese, Please!

This project helps youngsters recognize shapes and strengthens fine-motor skills! Place yellow triangle cutouts on a table along with hole punchers. Encourage students to punch holes in the triangles so they resemble slices of Swiss cheese. Have each child notice that the cheese is a triangle and yet the holes are circles. Encourage her to glue her cheese slices to a paper plate. Then display the plates with the mouse crafts from Friday's group-time activity (page 78).

Bubble Bath

✏️ Draw circles to make bubbles.

🖍️ Color.

Shapely Sea Life

Color by the code.

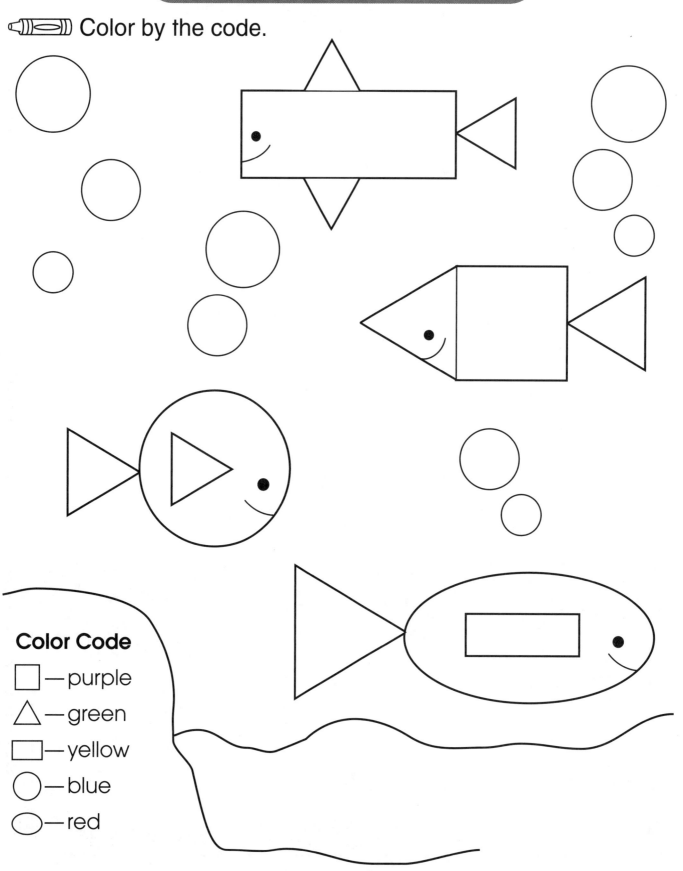

Color Code

☐—purple

△—green

▭—yellow

○—blue

⬭—red

Day-by-Day Math Plans • ©The Mailbox® Books • TEC61392

Shape Attributes

Centers for the Week

Set out craft foam shapes—such as triangles, squares, ovals, and circles—to provide some with straight edges only and some with a curved edge. Label one container with a straight line and one with a curved line. A youngster takes a shape and studies its attributes. Then she places it in the appropriate container.

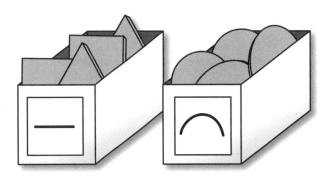

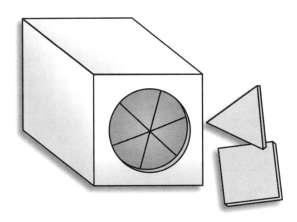

Gather a few shape manipulatives—such as a square, a triangle, and a circle—and place them in a feely box. A child reaches into the box and handles a shape. He feels its edges, guesses the shape, and removes it to see whether his guess is correct.

For this partner center, provide a copy of the triangle, square, rectangle, and circle cards from page 151. One child secretly chooses a shape and describes it to her partner. She gives clues such as the number of sides and corners, difference or sameness in lengths of the sides, and whether the edge is curved. The partner guesses the shape, and the classmate tells if the guess is correct. When the shape is correctly guessed, the partners switch roles.

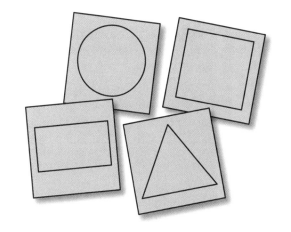

	Group Time	Math Talk
Monday	Show a triangle shape and discuss its three sides and corners. Then give each child a triangle cutout. Have her shout, "Hip hip hooray!" touching one side for each word she says. Repeat for each corner. ***Attributes of a triangle***	If you were playing outdoors and found two long sticks and two shorter sticks, what shape could you make? What if you found only three sticks? What shape could you make?
Tuesday	Place on a flannelboard several rectangles in different sizes, colors, and orientations. Point to each shape and have students describe its attributes. Then discuss how the size, color, and orientation may be different, but the sides and corners are what define the shape. ***Attributes of a rectangle***	Pretend you draw a shape in the sand that has a curved edge with no sides and no corners. What shape did you draw? What other shape might you draw? Describe the shape.
Wednesday	Form a square using four craft sticks. Prompt students to count each side as you touch it. Repeat with each corner. Add two sticks to make a rectangle. Encourage youngsters to describe how a rectangle is similar to and different from a square. ***Attributes of a square and rectangle***	Imagine you bought a new picture frame. It has four equal sides and four corners. What shape is the frame? What other shape might a picture frame be? Describe the frame's shape.
Thursday	Put different shape cards (page 151) in a bag. Have students pass the bag as you lead them in saying, "One, two, three, four—circles, triangles, squares, and more!" Prompt the child with the bag to show a card, name the shape, and describe its geometric attributes. Have him return the card to the bag and continue. ***Identifying and describing shapes***	Pretend you go shopping and buy snack crackers that have three sides and three corners. What shape are the crackers? Name other foods that have different shapes.
Friday	Describe the attributes of a particular shape and encourage youngsters to guess what it is. When the shape is guessed, draw it on a board or chart paper to verify the guess. ***Identifying shapes by attributes*** *It's a triangle.*	Imagine you wrote a letter and put it in an envelope. The envelope has two long sides, two shorter sides, and four corners. What shape is the envelope? You put a stamp that has four equal sides and four corners on the envelope. What shape is the stamp?

Projects and More!

Perfectly Square
(See the directions on page 86.)

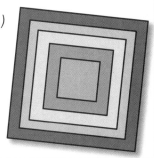

Gross-motor:
Arrange a class supply of shape cutouts in a circle. Then have students march around the circle. Ring a bell and prompt each child to stand by the nearest shape. Call out a shape, and then invite each child near that shape to hold it up. Call on a youngster to describe its attributes. Continue using other gross-motor movements.

Roaming Rectangles Booklet
(See the directions on page 86.)

Practice page:
See page 88 for practice with shape attributes.

Shape Mobile
(See the directions on page 86.)

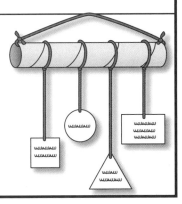

Bonus Ideas

Song:
Give each child a circle cutout. Discuss how a circle has a curved edge with no straight sides or corners. Then have youngsters trace the edge of their circles with their fingertips as you lead them in singing this song.

Round and Round
(tune: "The Muffin Man")

A circle goes around and round,
Around and round,
Around and round.
A circle goes around and round,
Because its edge is curved!

Rhyme:
No pencils or paper are needed to draw these squares! As you lead the group in saying the rhyme shown, encourage each child to draw a square in the air with his finger.

A square is fair; yes, it's true,
Four equal sides—four corners too!
You'll surely know this shape by name
When the corners and sides are all the same!

Perfectly Square

Give each child five paper squares in different colors and graduated sizes. Have her start with the largest square and then glue the next largest square to it as shown. Encourage her to continue gluing the remaining squares in size order from largest to smallest. As she works, remind her that, although the squares are different colors and sizes, they each have four corners and four equal sides.

Roaming Rectangles Booklet

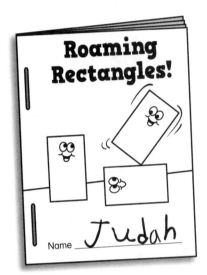

Materials for one project:
copy of page 87
three colorful 1¾" x 3" paper rectangles
glue
scissors
stapler

Steps:

1. For each page, read the text and then glue a rectangle to the box. Trace the edges of the rectangle with your fingertip, noticing the two longer sides, two shorter sides, and four corners.
2. Cut apart the booklet pages.
3. Stack the pages in order and staple them along the left side.

Shape Mobile

Materials for one project:
paper towel tube
tagboard shapes (circle, square, triangle, rectangle)
yarn
hole puncher
marker

Setup: Tie four lengths of yarn to the tube as shown.

Steps:

1. Trace the edge(s) of each shape with your finger, counting the number of sides and corners.
2. Dictate or write the number of sides and corners on each shape.
3. Punch a hole in each shape and then tie each one to a different length of yarn, with help as needed. *Teacher: Punch a hole in each end of the tube and attach a yarn hanger.*

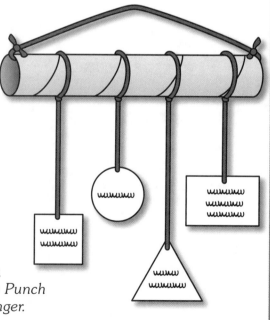

Roaming Rectangles!

Name _____

Day-by-Day Math Plans • ©The Mailbox® Books • TEC61392

This rectangle stands up.

1

This rectangle lies down.

2

This rectangle balances on the ground!

3

Name _____

Geometry
Shape attributes

Simple Shapes

 Trace.

Circle		Square	
curved edge 0 sides 0 corners	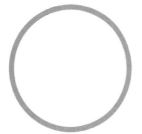	4 equal sides 4 corners	
Triangle		Rectangle	
3 sides 3 corners		2 long sides 2 short sides 4 corners	

Draw.

Day-by-Day Math Plans • ©The Mailbox® Books • TEC61392

Shapes in the Environment

Centers for the Week

Take photos (or cut pictures from magazines) of items with identical shapes, such as a round clock and a paper plate. Make several picture pairs to include other environmental shapes. Place the photos facedown. A child flips two photos. If the pictured items are the same shape, she sets the pair aside. If not, she turns them back over and the next player takes a turn.

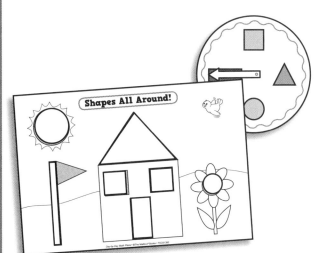

Make two copies of page 93. Provide two cutouts for each shaded shape on the page. Also, provide a spinner (pattern on page 149) programmed with the corresponding shapes. Two students visit the center. In turn, youngsters spin the spinner and place a cutout atop a corresponding shape. If a child spins a shape he does not need, his turn ends. Play continues until each child completes his page.

Trace several objects—such as a ruler, a square block, a round plastic lid, and a musical triangle—onto paper. Then conceal the items in a sack. A child reaches in the sack and handles an object. She guesses what the item is and then removes it to see if her guess is correct. Then she places the object atop the matching outline.

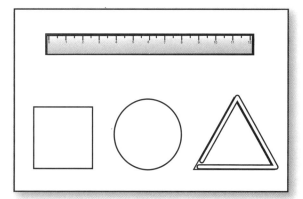

Group Time	Math Talk

Monday

For each child, draw a geometric shape on a sticky note. Encourage her to walk around the room and attach the note to an object that corresponds to the shape. Then discuss each youngster's choice and how the object relates to the shape. ***Recognizing environmental shapes***

Some signs in the environment are shaped like a rectangle, a triangle, a circle, and a square. Why do you think signs are different shapes?

Tuesday

Secretly notice an object whose shape corresponds to a geometric shape. Then use the shape name and positional words to help youngsters locate and identify the object. For example, you might say, "I see a large object shaped like a rectangle, and it's beside the bookshelf." Repeat with other objects. ***Identifying environmental shapes***

What shape is a bed? Why do you think a bed is shaped like a rectangle? Imagine your bed is shaped like a triangle. Would it be comfortable to sleep in? Explain.

Wednesday

For this small-group activity, show a book or magazine page and silently choose a pictured item that has a geometric shape. Say, for example, "I spy something shaped like a circle on this page." Then have students guess the secret item. ***Identifying environmental shapes***

Think about the wheels on a bicycle. What shape are they? Would wheels work if they were square? Why?

Thursday

Seat students in a circle. Set a timer and walk around the group carrying several craft foam shapes. When the timer goes off, drop a shape in the lap of a child you are standing near. Then encourage the child to name an environmental object similar to that shape. ***Naming geometric objects***

What shape is the seat on a park bench? Why do you think a bench is made with a rectangular seat?

Friday

Read aloud *The Shape of Things* by Dayle Ann Dodds. Review the last page with students and ask them to locate specific shapes in the illustration. ***Identifying environmental shapes***

What shape is a pizza? What other things are this shape?

Projects and More!

Big Book of Everyday Shapes

(See the directions on page 92.)

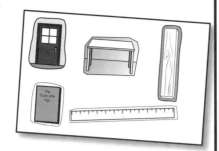

Partner game: Cut out desired shape cards from page 151. For each shape, program a blank card with a photo or magazine picture of a corresponding-shaped object. Place the card sets facedown in two separate rows. Have a child flip one card from each row. If the pictured object corresponds to the shape card, he sets the pair aside. If not, he turns them back over. Play continues, in turn, until all the cards are paired.

A Shapely Display

(See the directions on page 92.)

Jenna found a button. The button is a circle!

Practice page: See page 94 for practice with shapes in the environment.

Environmentally Abstract

(See the directions on page 92.)

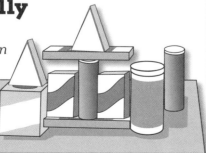

Bonus Ideas

Poem: Whether indoors or out, this poem about environmental shapes is sure to enhance students' observation skills! Encourage youngsters to pretend their hands are binoculars as you lead them in reciting the poem shown. Then invite children to name things not mentioned in the poem.

Shapes Are Everywhere!

Shapes, shapes—look all around.
There are many to be found.
Pillows, books, beds, and clocks,
Buttons, TVs, pizza, blocks.
Look down low; look up high!
Doors, windows, tables, pie.

Snack: Give each child assorted-shaped snack crackers. Say, "A [triangle] is a shape that could be a treat. Find a [triangle] for you to eat!" Have each child find her triangular cracker and eat it. Continue in the same way, replacing the underlined words with a different shape name.

Big Book of Everyday Shapes

This search-and-find project helps youngsters associate everyday objects with geometric shapes! Split the class into small groups. For each group, draw a different shape on a 12" x 18" sheet of paper. Give each group catalogs and magazines. Then have youngsters cut out catalog pictures that correspond to their shape. After verifying the choices, have students glue the pictures to the page. Bind the pages together to make a class book titled "Big Book of Everyday Shapes."

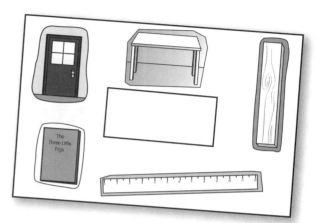

Jenna found a button.
The button is a circle!

A Shapely Display

Display several shapes. Encourage each child to find an object whose shape is similar to one of the displayed shapes. Then take a picture of her holding the object or standing near it. Have her glue the photo to colorful paper; then invite her to decorate around the photo with the corresponding craft foam shapes. Add text similar to that shown and display the projects for all to see!

Environmentally Abstract

With this collaborative project youngsters learn about shapes in the environment and create environmentally friendly artwork! Provide household recyclables that resemble assorted geometric shapes along with a sturdy sheet of cardboard and glue. Have small groups of students take turns to create an abstract structure. As children work, encourage them to tell how each item corresponds to a specific shape.

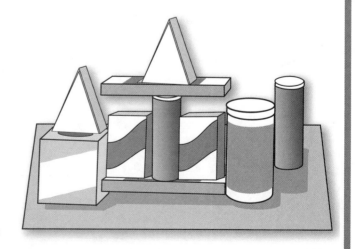

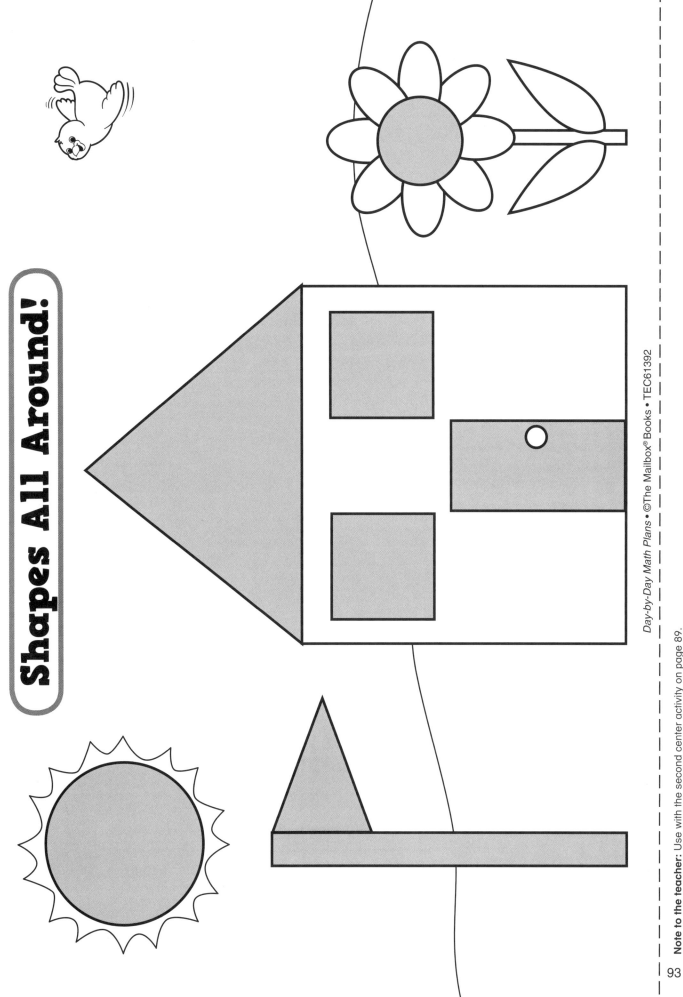

Shapes All Around!

Day-by-Day Math Plans • ©The Mailbox® Books • TEC61392

Note to the teacher: Use with the second center activity on page 89.

Name _____

94

What's Cooking?

 Color by the code.

Color Code

○ — red   △ — yellow

□ — orange   ▢ — blue

Day-by-Day Math Plans • ©The Mailbox® Books • TEC61392

Note to the teacher: Help the student color each shape in the color code; then have him use the code to color the picture.

Positional Words

Centers for the Week

Stage an area with objects to help youngsters practice positional words through movement. For example, provide a table to crawl *under*, a pillow to step *over*, a play tunnel (or box) to crawl *through,* a chair to walk *around* or sit *on*, and a plastic hoop to step *in* and *out* of. As they move, encourage students to make statements using positional words, such as "I'm crawling *under* the table!"

The horse is *in* the corral!

Put in your block area a toy barn along with farm animals and accessories. Elicit students' help in building a corral. Then invite them to engage in pretend farm play. As they play, encourage youngsters to use positional words while moving animals to different locations in relation to the barn and corral.

Provide a unique stuffed animal and introduce him as "Fred." Encourage one child to place Fred somewhere in the room and tell his partner, "Find Fred!" When the child finds Fred, have him describe his location using positional words, such as "Fred is *on* the bookshelf!" Then have youngsters switch roles.

Find Fred!

	Group Time	Math Talk
Monday	Give each child a green pom-pom (frog) and a brown paper strip (log). Announce directions, instructing youngsters to hop their frogs *on, off, behind, in front, over,* and *beside* the log. **Positional word knowledge**	Let's say you're walking to the library and see two houses on either side of it. Would you say the library is *behind, between,* or *in front* of the houses?
Tuesday	Place a teddy bear on a chair. Pretend you forgot where it is and say, "Teddy bear, teddy bear, where can you be?" prompting students to say, "The teddy bear is *on* the chair!" Continue in the same way, placing the bear in other positions in relation to the chair. **Appropriate use of positional words**	Imagine you take a family trip to the beach. Your brother runs toward the water, and you hear a big splash! Is your brother *in* or *out* of the water? What if he's swimming, but you can't see him? Is he *under* the water or *on top* of the water?
Wednesday	Set out a length of blue bulletin board paper (brook). Then announce actions such as "Step *in* the brook and splash your feet," "Step *out* of the brook," "Walk (tiptoe, march, or hop) *around* the brook," and "Jump *across* the brook without getting your feet wet!" **Positional word knowledge, gross motor, following directions**	Pretend a train is chugging down the tracks toward a tunnel. Using positional words (such as *in, through,* and *out*), describe what happens when the train reaches the tunnel entrance.
Thursday	Place kitten cutouts (patterns on page 99) around the room. Pretend you heard a kitten meow. Then lead students on a kitten hunt. Each time a kitten is found, prompt youngsters to name its location using a positional word. **Appropriate use of positional words, participating in a game**	Let's say you are standing close to a classmate. One of your shoulders is touching one of her shoulders. Would you say you're standing *behind* or *beside* the classmate? What if the *front* of your body is facing the *back* of her body? What is your position?
Friday	Read aloud *Chicka Chicka Boom Boom* by Bill Martin Jr. and John Archambault. Then post a tree cutout on a wall and give each child a die-cut letter. Have her use a small piece of Sticky-Tac adhesive to attach the letter *on, above, below,* or *beside* the tree. **Positional word knowledge, responding to a story**	Pretend it's raining. Would you hold your umbrella *in front of* or *above* your head? Why? When an umbrella is above your head, where is your body in relation to the umbrella?

Projects and More!

What Do You See?
(See the directions on page 98.)

Gross-motor:
For this outdoor activity, create an obstacle course that leads youngsters *in*, *out*, *over*, *under*, *up*, *down*, and *around* a variety of objects. Also obtain a whistle. Determine an appropriate length of time for the group to maneuver through the course; then encourage students to complete the course before you blow the whistle!

Where Is Bear?
(See the directions on page 98.)

Snack:
Use positional words to instruct students to make this snack. To make one, put a small graham cracker rectangle on a plate. Then spread green-tinted frosting on a vanilla wafer and place it above the cracker. Finally, put M&M's Minis candies on the frosting. What a lovely tree!

Practice page:
See page 100 for practice with positional words.

Bonus Ideas

Transition:
Have a child stand near you with his eyes closed. Place a beanbag *on* your head; then prompt him to open his eyes and tell the beanbag's location using an appropriate positional word. Send him on his way and continue, placing the beanbag in different locations.

Time filler:
Display an open box in front of the group. Position a child with her back to the box and hand her a stuffed toy. On your signal, have her toss the toy over her shoulder. Then have her turn around and tell whether the toy landed *in*, *behind*, *in front of*, or *beside* the box.

Project Time

What Do You See?

Give each child a piece of paper and encourage her to draw a wavy line lengthwise across the paper. Have her color the bottom of the paper blue so it resembles water. Next, read aloud the script below, pausing after each step to have her draw the appropriate items on her paper.

Script:

1. Water, water, what do you see? I see the sun shining right above me!
2. Sun, sun, what do you see? I see a fish swimming in the sea.
3. Fish, fish, what do you see? I see a shark close behind me!
4. Shark, shark, what do you see? I see a boat floating on the sea.
5. Boat, boat, what do you see? I see a child sitting in me!

Where Is Bear?

Materials for one project:

green or brown construction paper
disposable bowl (cave)
gray paint
paintbrush
green tissue paper
craft foam bear
glue

Setup: Cut a portion from the bowl so it resembles a cave entrance.

Steps:

1. Paint the cave gray; then glue it to the construction paper.
2. Glue crumpled tissue paper (bushes) to the construction paper.
3. When the project is dry, place the bear in different locations and describe its position in relation to objects in the scenery.

TEC61392

TEC61392

Name _____

Where Are They?

Listen and do.

Day-by-Day Math Plans • ©The Mailbox® Books • TEC61392

Note to the teacher: Help a child cut out the cards on a copy of this page. Have her glue the rabbit *in front* of the stump, the squirrel *on* the stump, the cat *in* the doghouse, the dog *beside* the house, the plane *above* the cloud, and the bird *below* the cloud. Then invite her to color the page.

100

Complex Shapes

Centers for the Week

Put a cube, a triangular pyramid, and a sphere-shaped object in a feely bag. Place a square, triangle, and circle cutout nearby. A child reaches in the bag, handles an object, and guesses whether it's a cube, a pyramid, or a sphere. He removes the three-dimensional object to check his guess; then he places the object with the corresponding two-dimensional shape.

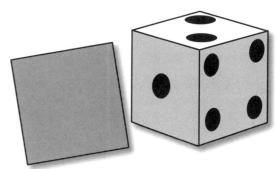

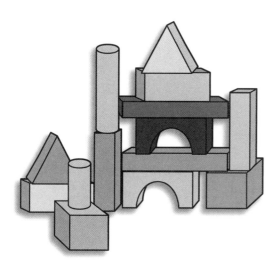

Set out a supply of building blocks that includes cylinders, rectangles, squares, and triangles. A student uses the blocks to build a structure. As she works, ask her to point to a block and name a two-dimensional shape that is part of the block. For example, she might say, "The top and bottom of a cylinder are circles!"

Provide play dough and wide-edged geometric cookie cutters. A child presses a cookie cutter into a thick lump of dough. He removes the three-dimensional shape from the cookie cutter and then flattens the dough so it resembles the two-dimensional shape. He repeats the process with other cookie cutters.

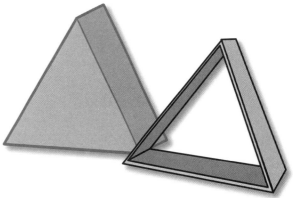

Group Time	Math Talk

Monday

Display a cone, a sphere, and a cube. Help students count the faces, edges, and corners of each shape. Discuss the similarities and differences; then have youngsters compare the three-dimensional shapes to corresponding two-dimensional shapes. *Analyzing and comparing two- and three-dimensional shapes*

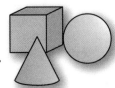

Imagine you got a new ball. You want your friend to guess what it is, so you give her a clue. Would you say your new toy is shaped like a sphere or a cube?

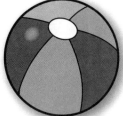

Tuesday

Pass around a few three-dimensional objects for students to view and handle. For each object, ask youngsters to predict whether it can roll, slide, or be stacked and explain why. Then test students' predictions and record the outcomes. *Predicting outcomes based on shape attributes*

If you want to sit on something, do you think it would be better to sit on a sphere-shaped object or a cube-shaped object? Explain.

Wednesday

Arrange chairs in a circle and put a copy of a three-dimensional shape card (page 151) under each chair. Play music as students walk around the chairs. Stop the music and prompt each child to sit in a chair and pick up the card. Name a shape, prompting each youngster with that shape to hold the card in the air. Have students return the cards and restart the music. *Recognizing three-dimensional shapes*

Let's say you decide to build a castle using triangular- and rectangular-shaped blocks. What shape blocks would you put at the bottom of the castle, and what shape would you put at the top? Why?

Thursday

Put a cutout copy of the cards on page 151 in a pocket chart with the cards facing away from the viewer. Have youngsters chant "two-D, three-D, what will it be? Flip a card, and we will see!" Flip a card and have students identify the featured shape as two- or three-dimensional. Continue in the same way. *Identifying two- and three- dimensional shapes*

If you were to describe the moon, what three-dimensional shape would you say it looks like? What about the sun? Can you name other things that are spheres?

Friday

Gather three-dimensional objects that correspond to the 3-D picture cards on page 151. Give each child a copy of a card. Display an object and prompt each child with a corresponding shape card to hold it in the air. Have the group identify the shape; then repeat the process. *Identifying three-dimensional shapes*

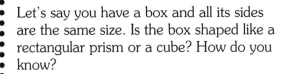

Let's say you have a box and all its sides are the same size. Is the box shaped like a rectangular prism or a cube? How do you know?

<table>
<tr><td>

Projects and More!

Solid Catch!
(See the directions on page 104.)

Outdoor activity: Gather playground balls and throwing discs and take youngsters outside. Ask students to tell which toy is a sphere and which is a circle. Then divide the class into groups and give each group a ball and a disc. Encourage youngsters to play with the items and notice similarities and differences in how they move.

Cylindrical Caterpillar
(See the directions on page 104.)

Practice page: See page 106 for practice with complex shapes.

Partner activity: Make two copies of the three-dimensional shape cards on page 151. Cut the cards apart and scatter them facedown. A child flips two cards and identifies each shape. If the cards match, he sets them aside. If they do not, he turns them back over. Play continues until all the cards are matched.

</td><td>

Bonus Ideas

Take-home activity: Make a copy of page 105 for each child. Before sending the assignment home, help students brainstorm three-dimensional objects that correspond to each shape on the page. Then encourage youngsters to have fun searching for three-dimensional objects with their families!

Rhyme: Help youngsters remember simple three-dimensional attributes with this fun rhyme!

3-D shapes are thick or tall.
They take up space, but that's not all!
3-D shapes are never flat.
They're solid shapes, and that is that!

</td></tr>
</table>

Project Time

Solid Catch!

Materials for one project:
large paper plate half
small foam ball (or Ping-Pong ball)
stickers
12" length of yarn
tape
hole puncher
hot-glue gun (optional, for teacher use only)

Steps:
1. Shape the plate half into a cone and then tape it in place.
2. Decorate the outside of the cone with stickers.
3. Punch a hole near the top of the cone and tie one end of the yarn to the hole.
4. Tape (or hot-glue) the ball to the loose end of the yarn. Then toss and catch!

Cylindrical Caterpillar

Materials for one project:
six 2" x 5" green construction paper strips
3" green construction paper circle
2 pipe cleaner pieces (antennae)
marker
tape
glue

Steps:
1. Form each strip into a loop and tape the ends together.
2. Tape the loops together to make a caterpillar body.
3. Draw a face on the circle and attach the antennae.
4. Glue the head to one end of the caterpillar body.

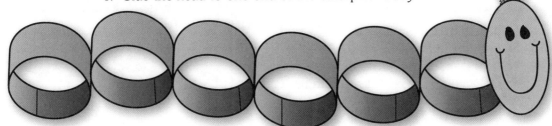

Dear Family,

Help your child find objects or pictures of objects that represent each three-dimensional shape. Have your child draw or glue a picture of each item in the appropriate box. Then help him or her label each picture with the name of the object. Have your child bring the page back to school by _____ to share with the class.

Have fun, and thanks for your help!

Sincerely, _____

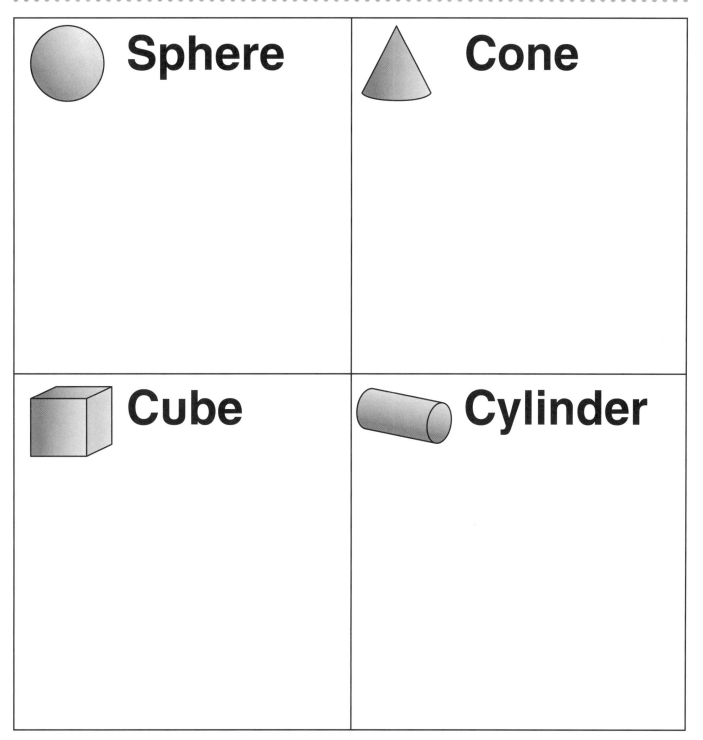

Sphere	Cone
Cube	**Cylinder**

Super Solids

 Circle.

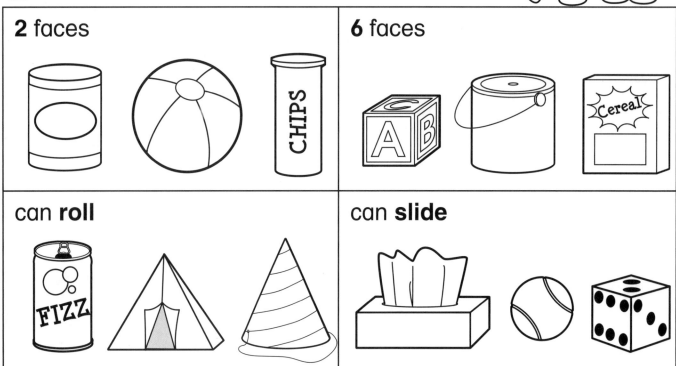

| **2** faces | **6** faces |
| can **roll** | can **slide** |

Look at each shaded face. Circle the shape name.

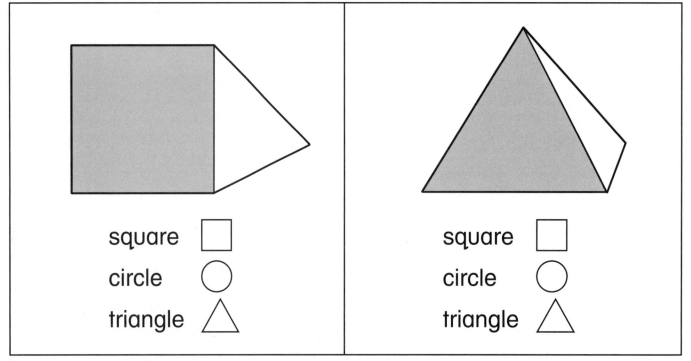

square □
circle ○
triangle △

square □
circle ○
triangle △

Working With Shapes

Centers for the Week

For this teacher-guided center, cut a copy of page 111 in half where indicated. Provide a square and a rectangle for tracing, along with paper and markers. Help students follow the step-by-step directions, pointing out the number of edges, faces, and corners in Step 6. Then ask, "How are a cube and rectangular prism the same?" "How are they different?"

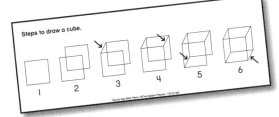

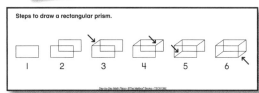

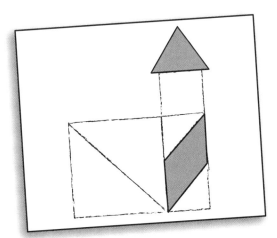

On separate sheets of paper, trace tangram shapes to create illustrations, such as a house, truck, and castle. Provide a supply of tangrams. A child chooses a drawing and places tangrams atop the matching shape outlines. When he's finished, he removes the shapes and re-creates the design beside the page.

Program a copy of the spinner on page 149 with different shapes. Provide paper and crayons. A child spins the spinner and draws the shape spun on paper. She continues in the same way, creating a design or picture as she works. For an easier version, replace the crayons with shapes that match the ones on the spinner. Then the child spins and places the appropriate manipulative on the paper.

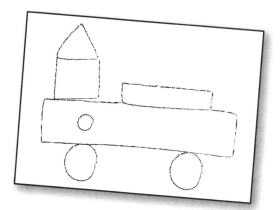

Group Time	Math Talk

Monday

Invite four children of about the same height to lie on the floor and form a square. Ask the group, "How can we change this square into a rectangle?" After youngsters offer ideas, invite more students to help transform the square into a rectangle. *Manipulating a shape to make a new shape*

Let's say you have a square piece of cake. You want to share it with a friend, so you cut the cake in half diagonally. What shape will each piece of cake be? What type of cake is your favorite?

Tuesday

Place a felt right triangle on a flannelboard. Hand a child an identical felt triangle and ask, "Can you join this triangle with the one on the board to make a rectangle?" When she's finished, ask her to change the rectangle back into a triangle. Repeat with two felt squares. *Putting together and taking apart shapes*

Pretend you want to make a card for someone's birthday. You take square paper and fold it in half. What shape is the folded paper? What shape envelope will you need for the card?

Wednesday

For this small-group activity, set out play dough and round-end toothpicks. Have each child roll small balls of dough and then connect several balls with toothpicks to form a specific shape. Encourage her to add or remove toothpicks and dough to make new shapes. *Making and manipulating shapes*

Imagine you're flying a diamond-shaped kite and the wind blows so hard it folds the kite in half. What shape would the folded kite be?

Thursday

Give each child a square napkin. Have him fold the napkin in half lengthwise and identify the new shape. Have him unfold the napkin to make a square and then identify that shape. Then have him fold the square diagonally to make a triangle and ask him to identify the shape. *Manipulating a shape to make new shapes*

What shape does a full moon resemble? If you look up at the night sky and see only half a moon, what shape do you see? What other shapes do you see in a night sky?

Friday

Share the wordless picture book *Changes, Changes* by Pat Hutchins. Then build a house from wood blocks. Invite a small group of students to transform the house into a fire engine. Continue with other groups and the remaining transformations shown in the story. *Responding to a story*

If you have two square crackers and place them side by side, what shape do the two crackers make? If you take two more crackers and place them directly below the first two crackers, what shape would the crackers be then?

Projects and More!

Shapely Art
(See the directions on page 110.)

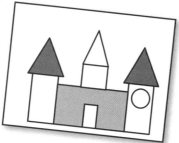

Partner activity:
Cut from craft foam two identical right triangles, squares, rectangles, and semicircles. On a sheet of paper, arrange each pair of shapes to form a new shape (*two triangles form a rectangle, two rectangles a square, and two semicircles a circle*); then trace around each new shape. Encourage the partners to assemble the pairs of shapes atop the outlines to form the new shapes.

Let's Build!
(See the directions on page 110.)

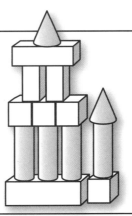

Practice page: See page 112 for practice working with shapes.

Shape Transformations
(See the directions on page 110.)

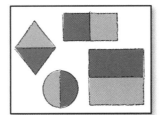

Bonus Ideas

Rhyme: For each child, cut a square in half diagonally. Place the resulting triangles in front of him to form a square. Then lead the group in performing this fun rhyme!

What's that shape—why it's a square!
   Point at the shape.
Do I see another shape there?
   Shrug your shoulders.
Cut the line so carefully.
   Pretend to cut with scissors.
Tell me now, what do you see?
Two triangles, easy as pie,
   Pick up the two triangles.
Cut from a square, my, oh my!
   Look surprised.
Put them back together, my friend,
   Join the triangles to make a square.
And just like that it's a square again!

Snack: Serve pretzel sticks and encourage each child to make a pretzel triangle. Then have him turn the triangle into a square and the square into a rectangle. After some shape-making practice, invite students to eat these tasty manipulatives!

Project Time

Shapely Art

This project goes from simple shapes to sensational artwork! Provide construction paper, glue, and assorted paper shapes in a variety of colors and sizes. Encourage each student to glue desired shapes to a sheet of paper to create an object or a picture.

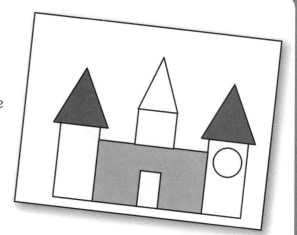

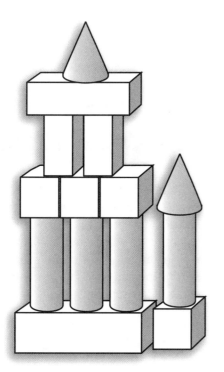

Let's Build!

Invite a small group of students to make a block sculpture, encouraging them to discuss each block's shape as they work. Snap a photo of the group with its finished sculpture and then have the students dismantle it. Repeat the process until everyone has had a chance to participate. Display the photos with the title "Building With Shapes."

Shape Transformations

Provide a plastic triangle, square, rectangle, and semicircle along with paper and crayons. Invite each child to trace a shape onto a sheet of paper. Prompt her to align the shape with the tracing and trace it again to form a new geometric shape. Then have her color each half of the new shape with a different-color crayon. Encourage her to repeat the process with the remaining shapes. Then help her mount the geometric masterpiece on a contrasting paper.

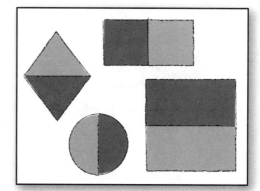

Steps to draw a cube.

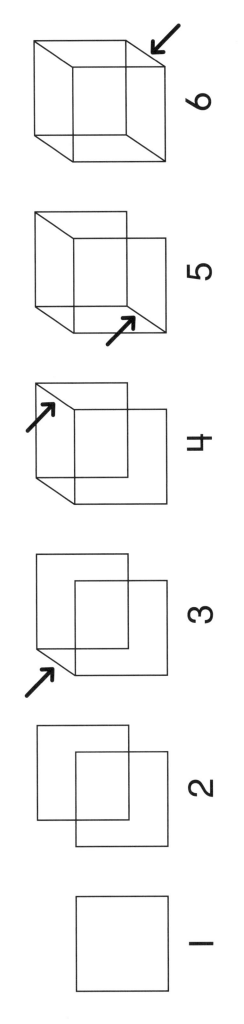

1 2 3 4 5 6

Steps to draw a rectangular prism.

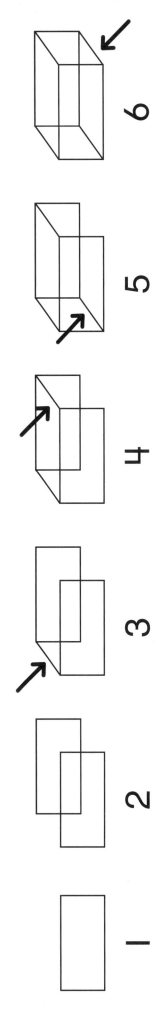

1 2 3 4 5 6

Note to the teacher: Use with the first center activity on page 107.

111

Balloon Tricks

Note to the teacher: Give each child a copy of the page. For each balloon, have her name the larger shape and then trace the outer lines.
Then have her trace the divider line and name each new shape. Finally, have her color the two halves different colors.

Copying and Extending Patterns

Centers for the Week

Glue pom-poms to tagboard strips to make patterns. Place the strips at a center along with a container of loose pom-poms. A youngster chooses a strip and places pom-poms below the strip to copy the pattern. Then, depending on his ability, he extends the pattern.

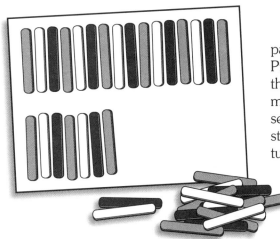

Glue colorful craft sticks to a sheet of construction paper. Make several sheets with different patterns. Provide a container of loose sticks. Two students visit the center and choose a paper. One child places a matching stick below the first stick in the pattern. A second child places a matching stick below the next stick in the pattern. The youngsters continue taking turns until the pattern has been copied and extended.

Make patterns with easily accessible manipulatives in your classroom and take a photo of each pattern. Enlarge the photos and place them at a center. Two youngsters select a photo and seek out the manipulatives. When they find the manipulatives used, they use them to make the pattern shown in the photo and then extend it.

Group Time	Math Talk	

Monday

Begin making a boy-girl-boy-girl pattern with several youngsters. Have the remaining students say the pattern with you as you point to each child and then help you extend the pattern. Repeat the activity with more complicated *ABB*, *AAB*, and *AABB* patterns. ***Extending patterns***

Pretend that you are scooping ice cream scoops on a cone and you're making a pattern of flavors. After the pattern is established, have a student pretend to scoop the next flavor in the pattern. Continue in the same way, encouraging students to imagine that the stack of scoops is getting taller and taller. Then have students explain the pattern.

Tuesday

Gather two different types of rhythm instruments and hand them out to youngsters. Take an instrument yourself and give an adult helper a different instrument. Demonstrate a simple *AB* sound pattern by playing the instruments. Then guide students to copy the pattern. Continue with *ABB* and *AAB* patterns. ***Copying patterns***

Clap your hands and pat your legs to make a pattern. Have students repeat the pattern and then explain the pattern to you. Continue with different patterns.

Wednesday

Gather a small group of students and give each child a plastic lidded container with several bear counters. Arrange your own bears to make a pattern and then have students copy your pattern with their bears. Check for accuracy. Then place your bears back in the container and secure the lid while students do the same. Have everyone shake their containers to mix the bears. Then play another round. ***Copying patterns***

Have students think of two of their favorite foods. Place a row of paper plates on the floor. Have the child touch the paper plates as she recites a pattern using those two foods. Pizza-chicken-pizza-chicken!

Thursday

Take youngsters for a walk through the school and outside, if possible. Have students look for man-made patterns and patterns in nature. (You may wish to scope out patterns ahead of time.) Consider looking for patterns on fences, buildings, windows, and flower gardens. ***Identifying patterns***

Tell students the following story: A man is building a row of houses, and he wants the houses to make a pattern. Ask students how he could accomplish his goal.

Friday

Make a pattern with desired manipulatives and have students study the pattern. Place a towel over the pattern and secretly remove a manipulative. Then remove the towel and have students identify the manipulative that is missing. Repeat the activity several times. ***Reading a pattern***

Tell students that you want your flower garden to have a pattern. Encourage youngsters to explain different ways you could make a pattern in a flower garden, such as using different colors, heights, or types of flowers.

Projects and More!	Bonus Ideas

Projects and More!

Wearable Patterns

(See the directions on page 116.)

Snack:
Give each child two different types of cereal (flat pieces work best) and a strip of paper. She arranges cereal pieces on the strip to make a pattern. After she reads her pattern aloud, she nibbles on her work.

Yum, Cookies!

(See the directions on page 116.)

Practice pages:
See pages 117 and 118 for practice extending patterns.

Splat!

(See the directions on page 116.)

Bonus Ideas

Rhyme:
Youngsters are sure to enjoy this active rhyme! Lead students in reciting the poem, stretching up toward the sky, and touching the ground appropriately to make a pattern. Continue with the verses shown.

Let's make a pattern, yes sirree!
Let's make a pattern—follow me!
[Up, down, up, down, up, down, up, down],
[Up, down, up, down, up, down, up, down].

Continue with the following: left and right *(sway to the left and to the right),* clap and pat *(clap hands and pat legs),* back and forth *(lean back and forth),* pat and stretch *(pat head and stretch arms upward)*

Song:
Gather manipulatives that can be made into a pattern and place them in a container. Sing the song with youngsters as you use the manipulatives to make a short pattern. Have a student copy the pattern with the manipulatives. Repeat the activity several times with different patterns.

(tune: "Clementine")

There's a pattern, there's a pattern,
There's a pattern on the floor!
Take a look and make a copy,
And then I will make some more!

Project Time

Wearable Patterns

Provide rubber stamps, ink pads, and paper strips. Have a child choose two rubber stamps. Use the stamps to begin a pattern on a strip. Then have him stamp to continue the pattern. When the ink is dry, staple the strip to make a headband.

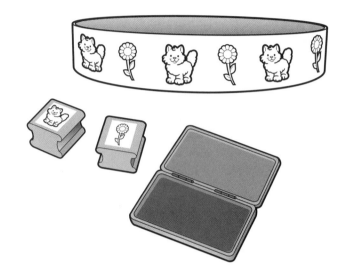

Yum, Cookies!

Gather several cookie cutters and prepare shallow pans of paint. Press cookie cutters in the paint and then make prints on a strip of paper to make a pattern. Continue with other cutters and patterns. Then let the resulting templates dry. Have a child choose a template and replicate the pattern on his own strip of paper.

Splat!

Put rice in several knee-high stockings and then tie them closed. Provide several shallow pans of paint. Have a child choose two different paint colors. Then hold a stocking by the knotted end and dip the rice-filled end into one of the colors. Bounce the stocking once on a strip of paper. Then repeat the process with a different stocking and the second color. Have the child repeat the process to make a pattern across the paper.

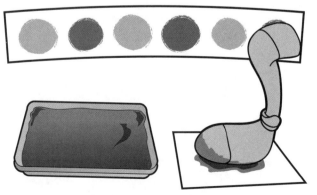

Name _____

At the Bakery

What comes next?
Circle.

Name

Patterns at the Pond

What comes next?

✂ Cut.

🧴 Glue.

Making Patterns

Centers for the Week

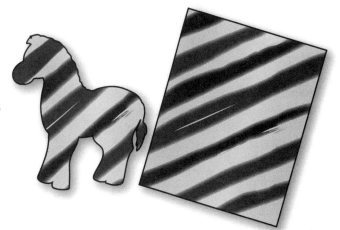

With this activity, youngsters can give a variety of animals patterned stripes! Provide paint and chunky paintbrushes. A child chooses two colors of paint and then paints patterned stripes on the paper. When the paint is dry, she traces an animal stencil onto the paper and cuts it out.

Place paper punches in a variety of shapes along with several different colors of paper at a table. A child punches shapes and then uses them to create a pattern.

Die-cut shapes from colorful paper and place them in a container. Provide a sand timer. Two youngsters flip the timer, and each child uses the shapes to make a pattern and extend it as far as possible. When the sand runs out, each student reads aloud his pattern and then counts the number of shapes. The child who has extended his pattern the farthest is the winner.

Group Time	Math Talk

Monday

Make several copies of the animal cards on page 123 and cut them out. Help a child make a pattern using the cards. Then encourage the remaining youngsters to read the pattern aloud, using the sounds the animals make. Continue for several rounds. Moo, baa, moo, baa! *Making patterns with sounds*

Imagine that a chef is making a huge cake for a very special birthday girl (or boy). The birthday girl wants to have patterned frosting flowers on the cake. What do you think the cake would look like?

Tuesday

Read aloud *Caps for Sale: A Tale of a Peddler, Some Monkeys and Their Monkey Business.* Then have each child draw a self-portrait at the bottom of a piece of paper. Have him make different-color fingerprints (caps) above his head in a desired pattern. Now he looks just like the peddler in the story! *Making patterns with colors*

Look around the classroom. What patterns do you see? (If youngsters have difficulty, guide them to look at specific areas.)

Wednesday

Get a container of linking cubes. Have a youngster link cubes to make a pattern. Have the remaining youngsters read her pattern aloud. Then challenge another child to use the same color cubes to build a different pattern. Finally, have the students take apart their patterns. Repeat the activity several times. *Generating different patterns*

Gather a container of pom-poms. Ask a child a question about her likes or dislikes, such as "What is your favorite pet?" After she answers, have a child choose a manipulative and place it on the floor. Have another youngster repeat the process, choosing a different color pom-pom. Then continue in the same way, having students make a pattern.

Thursday

Ask a child to strike a pose. Have another student strike a different pose. Encourage students to stand in a row and make a pattern using the two poses. Prompt the remaining students to read the pattern aloud. Repeat the activity with two (or three) different poses. *Making patterns with positions*

Pretend that you are frosting cookies. You want to make a pattern with your cookies. What are some ways you could do this?

Friday

Make a supply of tickets in two colors and give each child a ticket. Ask a student to imagine what the tickets are for. Then have students line up for the imaginary event, prompting them to make a pattern with their tickets. Play several rounds of this game, encouraging students to name different events. *Making patterns with colors*

You are decorating a snowman and want his buttons to show a pattern. What items would you use, and in what order would you attach them?

Projects and More!	Bonus Ideas

Handprint Patterns
(See the directions on page 122.)

Snack: Give each child a variety of crackers in two (or three) different shapes. Each child arranges his crackers on a paper towel to make a pattern. Then he eats his creation.

Patterns Galore!
(See the directions on page 122.)

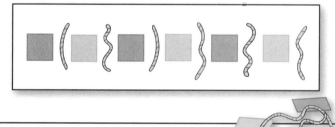

Practice Page
(See page 124 for patterning practice.)

My Personal Pattern
(See the directions on page 122.)

My pattern goes like this: chair, block, chair, block, chair, block.

—Mia

Song: Get different types of manipulatives and gather youngsters around. Place two rows of manipulatives on the floor: one that shows a pattern and one that does not. Then lead students in singing the song. Next, have students identify which row shows a pattern.

(tune: "Clementine")

Where's the pattern?
Where's the pattern?
Can you show me
Where it is?
Is it this one?
Is it that one?
Can you show me
Where it is?

Song: Gather colorful manipulatives. Have a child choose two colors of manipulatives and create an *AB* pattern. Then lead students in singing the song shown, inserting the appropriate colors.

(tune: "Are You Sleeping?")

[Red] and [yellow],
[Red] and [yellow],
[Red] and [yellow],
[Red] and [yellow].
You have made a pattern!
You have made a pattern!
[Red] and [yellow],
[Red] and [yellow].

Project Time

Handprint Patterns

Prepare shallow pans of paint. Have each child choose his two favorite colors and press a hand in each color. Then have him make an *AB* pattern by making handprints on a strip of paper.

Patterns Galore!

Provide a variety of craft materials, such as tissue paper squares, yarn pieces, ribbon pieces, and pom-poms. Have each child glue items to a wide strip of paper to make a pattern. When the glue is dry, staple the papers together with a cover titled "Patterns Galore!" Then place the resulting book in your reading center. Youngsters will love to read and touch the patterns.

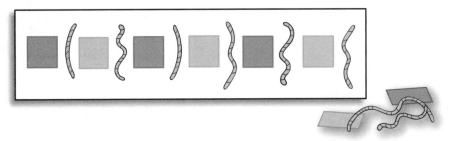

My Personal Pattern

To make this project, choose two sets of items in the classroom. For example, chairs and blocks, teddy bear counters and scissors, or markers and crayons. Place the items on the floor to make a pattern. Then take a photograph of the pattern. Attach the photo to a sheet of paper and write information about your pattern.

My pattern goes like this: chair, block, chair, block, chair, block.

—Mia

TEC61392

TEC61392

TEC61392

TEC61392

TEC61392

TEC61392

Name _____

Zoo-Time Patterning

✂ Cut.

🍶 Glue to finish each pattern.

Day-by-Day Math Plans • ©The Mailbox® Books • TEC61392

Exploring Length

Centers for the Week

Display a carrot, a baby carrot, a celery stalk, a pretzel rod, and a banana. Provide tagboard strips the length of each individual item. A child takes a strip and compares its length to that of each item, stopping when he finds an item that matches the strip in length. He sets the strips and item aside and repeats the process with each remaining strip.

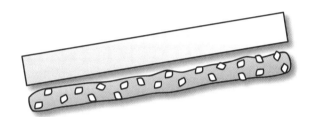

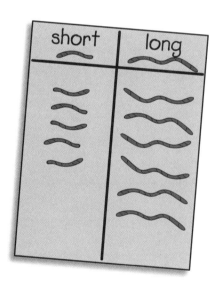

Divide and label brown poster board (garden) as shown. Cut brown yarn into long and short lengths (worms); then glue an appropriate-size worm below each heading. A student wiggles a worm onto the garden and compares its length to that of each worm. Then she places the worm in the appropriate column. She continues until all the worms have wiggled their way onto the garden.

Gather several pairs of different items that are the same length, such as a book and a block. Place one of each pair in a bag and display the remaining items. A child takes an object from the bag and compares its length to the length of the displayed items. When he finds a match, he sets the pair aside. Then he continues with each remaining item.

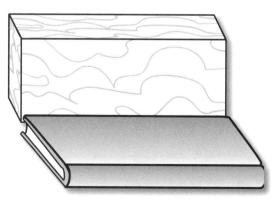

	Group Time	Math Talk	
Monday	Lay a towel on the floor and invite a child to stand by it. Ask, "If [child's name] lies on the towel, will he be longer than, shorter than, or the same length as the towel?" After youngsters respond, have him lie on the towel to determine the answer. Repeat with other students. ***Comparing length***	Which is shorter: a hammer or a nail? Which is longer: a screwdriver or a screw? Can you think of other tools that might be longer than a screwdriver?	
Tuesday	Have two or more children stand on a masking tape line. Prompt the group to chant, "One, two, three, four. Leap across the classroom floor!" Prompt the youngsters to leap forward; then use yarn to measure and compare the length of each child's leap. ***Nonstandard measurement, comparing length*** One, two, three, four. Leap across the classroom floor!	Which is longer: a car or a bus? Which is shorter: a bus or a train? Do you think more people would fit on a bus or a train? Explain.	
Wednesday	Give each child a length of thick yarn. Call on a student to place her yarn on the floor and have a classmate place his yarn next to hers. Then ask the group to compare the yarn lengths. Continue with two different lengths of yarn. ***Comparing length***	If three people want to sit together, should they sit on a sofa or on a chair? Explain.	
Thursday	Draw two snakes on each of several cards. Put the cards in a bag. Play music as students pass the bag around the circle. Stop the music and prompt a child to take a card and tell if one snake is longer than the other or if they're the same length. If the group agrees, youngsters hiss like snakes. If not, they sit quietly. Repeat. ***Participating in a game, comparing length***	Place your hand against the bottom of your foot. Which is longer: your hand or your foot? If you place the palms of your hands together, is one hand shorter than the other? Name a body part that is longer than your arm.	
Friday	Gather items that are longer than, shorter than, and the same size as a ruler. Invite a child to pick an item. Display a ruler and have her estimate whether the item is longer than, shorter than, or the same length as the ruler. Then help her compare the length of the object to that of the ruler. ***Comparing length***	Which is shorter: a marker or a sheet of paper? Which is longer: a brand-new pencil or a crayon? Is it possible for a pencil to be shorter than a crayon? Explain. 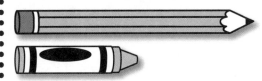	

Projects and More!

Friendly Footprints
(See the directions on page 128.)

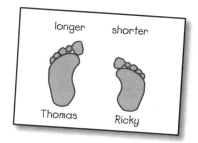

Partner activity:
Cut drinking straws to make an even number of pieces and put them in a bag. Each child takes a straw piece from the bag. They compare the lengths of the two straws, and the child with the longer one keeps them both. If youngsters draw the same-size straws, they return them to the bag. Play continues until the bag is empty.

Sparkling Sunshine
(See the directions on page 128.)

Practice pages:
See pages 129 and 130 for practice exploring length.

Crafty Windsock
(See the directions on page 128.)

Bonus Ideas

Transition:
Call on two children. Have each child place the palm of one hand against the palm of the other child's hand. Encourage the pair to compare their hands to see if one person's hand is longer or shorter than the other's or if their hands are the same length. Then have them hold hands and line up!

Rhyme:
Have youngsters sit in small groups. Give each group two classroom objects. Lead students in singing the song shown and then encourage each group to compare the items. After students discuss their items, collect them and pass a different pair of items to each group.

(tune: "Are You Sleeping?")

Is one longer?
Is one shorter?
Or are they
The same size?
Let's all take a look now.
Let's all take a look now.
Use your eyes.
Use your eyes.

Project Time

Friendly Footprints

Provide construction paper, paint, and hypoallergenic baby wipes. Invite two children at a time to join you. Have each student remove one shoe and sock. In turn, help each child paint the bottom of his foot and press it on one side of a sheet of paper. Then help him clean his foot with a wipe. Ask the two students to determine whether one footprint is longer or shorter than the other or if the prints are the same length. Then label the project with the students' names and the outcome.

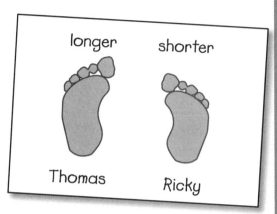

Sparkling Sunshine

Materials for one project:
blue construction paper
yellow construction paper circle
5 long and 5 short yellow construction paper triangles (sun rays)
yellow glitter
markers
glue

Steps:
1. Glue the circle (sun) to the middle of the paper.
2. Determine the long sun rays from the short ones. Then glue the rays around the sun, alternating them as shown.
3. Draw facial details on the sun, if desired.
4. Dab glue on the sun and sprinkle glitter on the glue. Shake off any excess glitter.

Crafty Windsock

Give each child a 9" x 12" sheet of construction paper. Provide colorful self-adhesive craft foam shapes and crepe paper streamers in two different lengths. Invite her to decorate the paper with shapes. Then help her form the paper into a cylinder and staple it in place. Have her notice the different streamer lengths and then glue the streamers to the bottom edge of the cylinder, encouraging her to alternate the lengths. Attach a yarn hanger to the project.

Name _____

Slithering Snakes

Color the **longer** snakes.

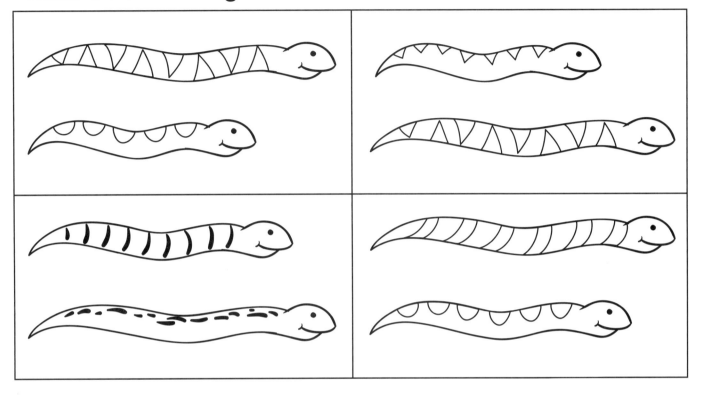

Color the **shorter** snakes.

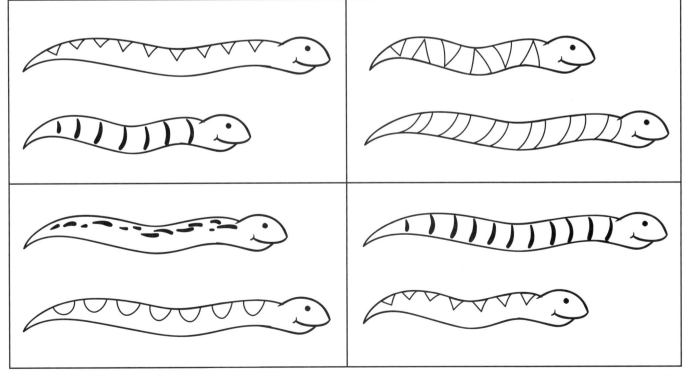

Ready to Draw

Cut out the [□□□□□□□].
Use it to measure.

Write.

_____ erasers

_____ erasers

| 0 | 1 | 2 | 3 | 4 | 5 | 6 |

_____ erasers

_____ erasers

_____ erasers

Exploring Weight

Centers for the Week

Put a balance scale at a center along with several different objects for weighing. A youngster investigates the balance scale and uses it to weigh different combinations of objects. Encourage students to describe the outcome of each weight investigation by using the terms *lighter, heavier,* or *same.*

Draw a house and a leaf on individual sheets of construction paper. Then put the papers at a center with an assortment of picture cards for sorting. A child puts cards showing items that are heavy on the house mat or light on the leaf mat. If he is unsure about the weight of a pictured item, he sets the card aside. For a more challenging center, provide a third sorting mat that shows a drawing of a rock. Vary the assortment of picture cards daily.

Wrap each of three same-size boxes in a different color of paper, wrapping the lids separately. Next, choose three types of items of various weights, such as craft feathers, counters, and catalogs. Store a few of each item inside a different box, making sure the weights of the boxes are substantially different. Put the boxes at a center. A youngster compares the boxes' weights by lifting each one. Next, she arranges the boxes from lightest to heaviest. Then she peeks inside each box to find out why the boxes are different weights.

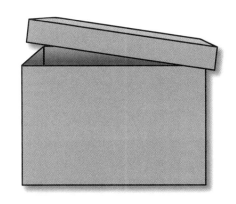

Group Time	Math Talk

Monday

Get a balance scale, a scooper, and individual containers of easy-to-scoop materials. Add a scoopful of material to one side of the scale. Ask students how to balance the scale and then follow through with one or more ideas. Have students use the terms *lighter*, *heavier*, and *balanced* to describe what happens. Repeat with varying materials and amounts. ***Investigating weight***

Imagine you are visiting a farm. What animals do you see? Which farm animal do you think weighs the most? Why? Which farm animal do you think weighs the least? Are there two animals that you think weigh about the same?

Tuesday

Get a supply of building blocks. Hand one block to each of two students. Tell each to return with a classroom object that is lighter or heavier than the block he has. Have him share his discovery with the class, allowing his classmates to compare the weights of his two objects. ***Comparing weights***

Have you ever seen something get weighed at a grocery store? Where else do people, animals, or objects get weighed? Why do you think these things are weighed?

Wednesday

Put 20 of the same object in a resealable plastic bag. Prepare three more bags with different objects. Show students two bags and ask them to predict which bag is heavier. Put the bags on opposite ends of a balance scale so youngsters can check their predictions. Continue with different combinations of bags. Remind students that each bag contains the same number of items. Ask students what this tells them about the items inside the bags. ***Predicting weight***

The weights of some things do not change. The weights of other things do change. What are some things that keep the same weight? What are some things that change weight? Why do you think some things change weight and other do not?

Thursday

Name and point to a classroom object. If a student thinks the object is heavy, she puts her hands on her knees. If she thinks the object is light, she puts her hands on her shoulders. A student who is unsure how to categorize the object's weight keeps her hands at her sides. Talk with youngsters about the weight of the object; then repeat the process. ***Recognizing weight***

Pretend you have been asked to move a big bag of potatoes. You try to lift the bag, but you can't. What other ideas do you have for moving the bag?

Friday

Read aloud *Who Sank the Boat?* by Pamela Allen. In this story, five animal friends go for a row in the bay. During a second reading of the tale, switch the boarding order so that a different critter sinks the boat. Then ask students, "Why did the boat sink this time?" ***Reasoning with weight***

What do you think this sentence means? "Fran acts as if she's carrying the weight of the world on her shoulders."

Projects and More!

Silly Seesaw

(See the directions on page 134.)

Gross Motor:
First, have students imagine they are very large and heavy elephants. Then invite them to move around, pretending to be this animal. Ring a bell to stop the movement. Continue the process by inviting students to imagine they are animals of varying weights.

Lighter and Heavier

(See the directions on page 134.)

Practice Page

(See page 136 for practice with exploring weight.)

A Weighty Collage

(See the directions on page 134.)

Bonus Ideas

Rhyme: Add a touch of dramatic flair to this upbeat poem! Have students use high, whispery voices when saying lines that name light objects and deep, loud voices when repeating lines that name heavy objects.

Light as a Feather
Light as a feather, light as a bee,
Light as a butterfly, light as a key.
Heavy as an elephant, heavy as a train,
Heavy as a dinosaur, heavy as a plane.
Everything has weight, yes sirree.
Heavy as a dump truck, light as a flea!

Rhyme: Before leading students in this rhyme, name two rhyming objects and invite students to decide which one is heavier. At the end of the rhyme, ask students to describe the weights of the two objects. Then continue with a different rhyming pair.

Weighing In
Some things are heavy;
Others are not.
A [rock] is heavy,
But a [sock] is not.
If something isn't heavy,
Then is it light?
That's a great question.
Let's decide!

Continue with the following:
bear, hair; pig, twig; rug, bug; ship, chip; tree, flea

Silly Seesaw

Materials for one project:
two 3" paper squares
small paper triangle
1" x 9" paper strip
9" x 12" manila paper
crayons
glue

Steps:

1. Glue the triangle and the paper strip to the manila paper to make a seesaw as shown.
2. Draw a heavy object on one paper square and a light object on the other.
3. Glue the picture of the heavier object to the lowered end of the seesaw and glue the picture of the lighter object to the raised end.
4. Add colorful details.

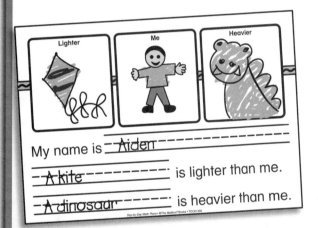

Lighter and Heavier

Whether you read this class-made book to the group or youngsters read the book with partners, the concepts of lighter and heavier are sure to be reinforced! Make a copy of page 135 for each child. A student draws himself in the box labeled "Me" and then draws one object lighter than himself and one object heavier than himself in the provided boxes. He writes his name to complete the first sentence on his page. Next, he writes (or dictates for you to write) the names of items he drew to complete the remaining sentences. Bind the students' pages into a class book titled "Lighter and Heavier."

A Weighty Collage

Use this collage project to reinforce the concept that all objects have weight. Provide picture cutouts (from magazines, newspaper fliers, or online) of things that are heavy, light, or in between. Ask a child to select several pictures. Next, help him glue the pictures collage-style onto construction paper. Guide the youngster to talk about his project using the terms *heavy, heavier, light,* and *lighter.*

Lighter	Me	Heavier

My name is _____

_____ is lighter than me.

_____ is heavier than me.

Day-by-Day Math Plans • ©The Mailbox® Books • TEC61392

Note to the teacher: Use with "Lighter and Heavier" on page 134.

Heavy and Light

 Color 😊 or ☹.

Are both things **heavy**?		Are both things **light**?	
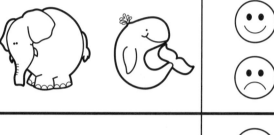	😊 ☹	 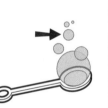	😊 ☹
	😊 ☹		😊 ☹
 	😊 ☹	 	😊 ☹
	😊 ☹		😊 ☹
	😊 ☹		😊 ☹

Bonus: Draw a classroom object that is **heavy**. Then draw a classroom object that is **light**.

Sorting Collections

Centers for the Week

Set out a copy of page 157. Provide a supply of three different kinds of craft foam shapes, such as stars, hearts, and flowers. A child places a different kind of shape in each section of the mat. She sorts the remaining shapes accordingly and then counts and compares the number of shapes in each section.

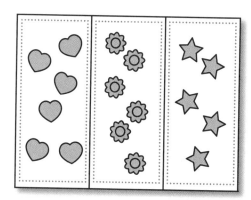

Draw and label two parking lots as shown. Place an appropriate-size car by each heading and provide corresponding-size cars for each lot. A child chooses a car and determines the appropriate lot according to the size of the car. Then he "drives" the car onto that lot. He continues with each remaining car.

Provide craft supplies in three different colors. Place 12" x 18" sheets of construction paper in coordinating colors at the center. A child visits the center and chooses a craft supply. Then he places it on the appropriate paper and glues it in place. He continues, sorting several craft items.

Group Time	Math Talk
Monday Place brown paper (land) and blue paper (water) on the floor. Give each child a copy of a card from page 141. Have him identify the vehicle, tell if it travels by land or water, and place the card on the appropriate paper. After all the cards are sorted, help students count and compare the results. ***Sorting by type, counting, comparing***	Imagine you help deliver animals to a zoo and a farm. Where would you take an elephant, a horse, and a giraffe? What about a lion, a goat, and a cow? How about a pig, a monkey, and a polar bear? 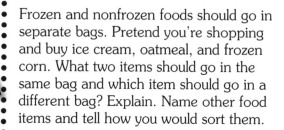
Tuesday Cut out a class supply of several different shapes and give one to each child. Set a timer and encourage youngsters to sort themselves into groups by shape before the timer goes off. Then help students count and compare the groups. ***Sorting by shape, counting, comparing***	Frozen and nonfrozen foods should go in separate bags. Pretend you're shopping and buy ice cream, oatmeal, and frozen corn. What two items should go in the same bag and which item should go in a different bag? Explain. Name other food items and tell how you would sort them.
Wednesday Post a drawing of a refrigerator and one of a pantry. Put containers from refrigerated and pantry foods in a grocery bag. Invite volunteers, in turn, to take an item from the bag and place it by the appropriate drawing. After all the food is "put away," help students count and compare the results. ***Sorting by type, counting, comparing***	Pretend you have one box labeled "summer clothes" and another labeled "winter clothes." How would you sort mittens, shorts, and a wool hat? What about flip-flops, a scarf, and a tank top? How about a sweater, a swimsuit, and a heavy jacket?
Thursday Ask each child to bring a teddy bear to school. (Have extras just in case!) Set out three different boxes. Have each child decide which box best fits her bear. Then have her place the bear near that box. Help students count and compare the number of bears in each group. ***Sorting by size, counting, comparing***	Imagine you're sorting hard and soft items onto two separate trays. Where will you put a rock, a pom-pom, and a cup? How about a feather, a ruler, and a cotton ball? What about a wood block, a washcloth, and a key? Name other hard and soft items and tell how you would sort them.
Friday Gather two groups of items, like toys and office supplies. Add two distracter items, such as a mitten and a fork. Put one item from each group in separate toy hoops. Display an item and have students decide which hoop it belongs in. Then display a distracter item. After confirming it doesn't belong in either hoop, set the item aside. Continue. ***Sorting by type, discriminating***	Pretend you have one basket labeled "fruits" and another labeled "vegetables." Where would you put an apple, a carrot, and a pear? How about a potato, an ear of corn, and an orange? Name other fruits and vegetables and tell how you would sort them.

Projects and More!

Sticky Shape Mobile
(See the directions on page 140.)

Partner activity:
Provide two laundry baskets and a pile of white and colorful clothing. Invite two children to pretend they're doing laundry. Encourage them to sort the pieces of clothing into the baskets. Then have the partners count and compare the amount of clothing in each basket.

Magnetic Puff Frame
(See the directions on page 140.)

Practice page:
See page 142 for practice with sorting.

Gross motor:
Arrange the class in two lines. Provide each team with a container of pom-poms in three colors. Get paper to match each color and place it a distance away from each team. On your signal, the first child on each team takes a pom-pom, runs and places it on a matching-color paper, and then runs back to his team. Play continues until all the pom-poms are sorted.

Bonus Ideas

Cleanup:
When cleanup time is over, place any miscellaneous items in a collection tub. At the end of the day, invite a child to be the Super Sorter. Encourage him to sort the items and return them to their proper places.

Snack:
Give each child a napkin and a cupful of colorful fruit-flavored cereal rings. Encourage her to sort the cereal onto the napkin in different color groups. When the sorting is done, invite her to eat her colorful treat!

Sticky Shape Mobile

Materials for one project:
plastic lid
3 shape cutouts, such as a heart, star, and flower
collection of self-adhesive craft foam shapes that match the cutouts
hole puncher
ribbon

Setup: Punch three holes at the bottom of the lid and one at the top. Punch a hole in each cutout.

Steps:
1. Sort the craft foam shapes into separate piles.
2. Peel the backing from each shape and attach the shape to a corresponding cutout.
3. Attach some shapes to the lid.
4. Tie one end of a length of ribbon to each cutout; then tie the loose end of the ribbon to a hole in the lid.
5. Tie a ribbon hanger to the top of the lid.

Magnetic Puff Frame

Materials for one project:
4 jumbo craft sticks
collection of 4 colors of pom-poms
tacky glue
strip of magnetic tape

Steps:
1. Glue the craft sticks together to make a frame.
2. While the glue sets, sort the pom-poms according to color.
3. Glue one color of pom-pom to each side of the frame.
4. Attach the magnetic tape to the back of the frame.

TEC61392

TEC61392

TEC61392

TEC61392

TEC61392

TEC61392

TEC61392

TEC61392

TEC61392

Happy Habitat

✂ Cut. Sort. 🧴 Glue.

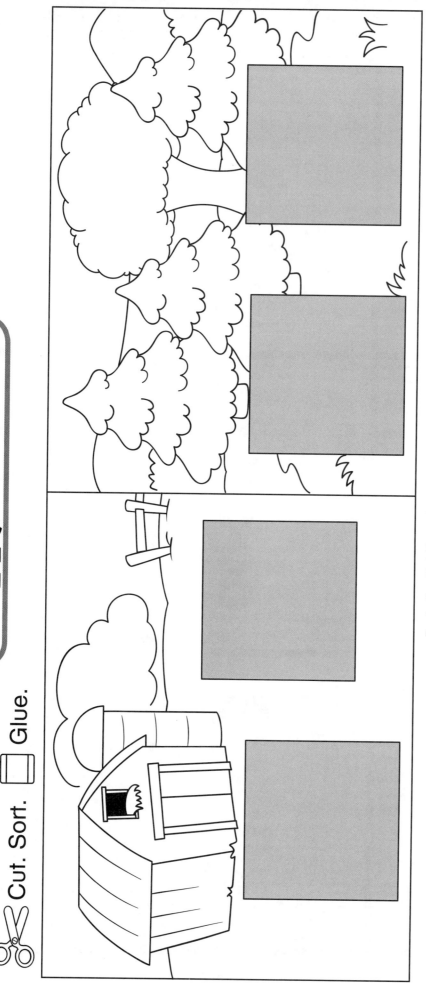

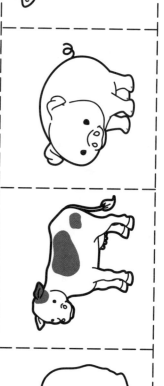

Day-by-Day Math Plans • ©The Mailbox® Books • TEC61392

Graphing

Centers for the Week

Provide a large graph with two columns labeled as shown and a variety of large and small stuffed animals. A student arranges the animals on the graph. Then she counts the animals in each column.

Place a variety of objects that either float or sink near a tub of water. Laminate a two-column graph labeled as shown. A child places an object in the water and observes whether it floats or sinks. Then she places it in the appropriate column. She continues with each object.

Place a class supply of simple graph paper at a table. (An Internet search of graph paper will turn up many options.) Mix up to four different types of cereal in a bowl. Provide a quarter-cup scooper. A child takes a scoop of cereal and places it on a napkin. He sorts the cereal into piles. Then he places the types of cereal in separate columns on a sheet of graph paper. Finally, he nibbles on his data.

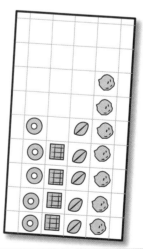

	Group Time	Math Talk
Monday	Read two different stories aloud. Then ask youngsters to think about which is their favorite. Display a two-column graph and label the columns with the story names. Have each child place a sticky note on the graph to show her favorite story. Then guide students to discuss the results. ***Reading a graph, counting, comparing numbers***	Tell students that several people were asked whether they liked rainy weather or sunny weather better. A graph was made of their opinions, and it turns out that a lot of people liked rainy weather! Why would people enjoy rainy weather?
Tuesday	Before group time, print out a large photo of each child. Then use the photos to help students graph themselves by hair color. (It's simple to place the photos on the floor in rows without using an actual chart.) ***Making a graph***	Ask, "If we made a graph of our favorite desserts, what type of desserts would we need to include?" Have students give suggestions. Then, if desired, draw a simple graph on your board and complete it using students' initials.
Wednesday	Gather the photos used for Tuesday's group-time activity. Have each child identify his own eye color. Then help students use the photos to graph eye color similar to the way they graphed hair color. ***Making a graph***	What question would you like to graph answers to? How would you make your graph?
Thursday	Place a two-column graph on the floor. Put two different types of manipulatives into a bag and place one of each type of manipulative on the graph to label each column. Have a child draw a manipulative from the bag and place it in the correct column. Continue with each child. Then discuss the results shown on the graph. ***Reading a graph, counting, comparing numbers***	I want to know how many students in this class like broccoli and how many do not, but I don't want to make a graph. What's another way for me to find out this information?
Friday	Gather student name cards. Make a two-column graph and label the columns "*M*" and "No *M*." Have students place their name cards in the appropriate columns to show whether their name has or does not have an *M*. Repeat the activity with different letters as time allows. ***Recognizing letters, making a graph***	I want to make a graph that shows our favorite things to do during the winter. What are some things I could put on my graph?

Projects and More!

Daily Weather Journal

(See the directions on page 146.)

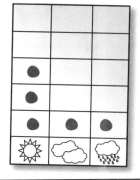

Snack: Give each child a spoonful of M&M's Minis candies and a simple empty graph. Have each child graph his candies by color. Then have him nibble on his treat.

Hot and Cold

(See the directions on page 146.)

Practice Page

(See page 148 for graphing practice.)

At the Pet Shop

(See the directions on page 146.)

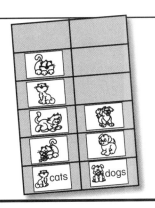

Bonus Ideas

Song: Lead students in singing the song. Then ask a question, such as "Have you ever been on an airplane?" Guide students in graphing the results.

(tune: "Clementine")

We are graphing.
We are graphing.
What's the first thing that we do?
First, we need to ask a question.
It is fun for me and you.

Song: Display a floor graph and place a title card on it labeled "Favorite Picnic Food." Label the columns "Hot Dogs," "Hamburgers," "Potato Chips," and "Other." Lead students in singing the song. Then discuss the different parts of the graph. Finally, have a child put a sticky note in a column to show her favorite picnic food.

(tune: "Twinkle, Twinkle, Little Star")

It is time to graph with me.
Take a look. What do you see?
There's the title,
Columns too.
Let's all find out what to do.
It is time to graph with me.
Take a look. What do you see?

Daily Weather Journal

Give each child a simple weather graph, such as the one shown. For each day throughout the week, have students identify the weather and then use bingo daubers to mark the appropriate columns on their graphs. At the end of the week, discuss the results shown on the graph. Then have youngsters take their graphs home.

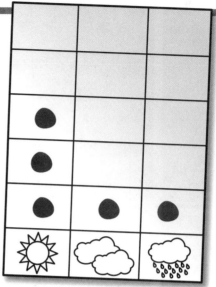

Hot and Cold

Here's a fun graphing project that gives little ones a fine-motor workout! Give each child a sheet of construction paper labeled as shown to make a two-column graph. Then give the youngster a grocery store flier. Have him cut out and glue pictures to his graph for a predetermined amount of time. Then discuss his graph using the words *more*, *fewer*, and *equal*.

At the Pet Shop

Give each child a copy of the cards on page 147 and a blank construction paper graph. Tell her that these are the animals available at the Perfect Paws Pet Shop. Have her cut out the cards and attach them to the graph to find out how many dogs and cats are available for purchase. Finally, discuss the results shown on the graph.

cats

TEC61392

dogs

TEC61392

TEC61392

TEC61392

TEC61392

TEC61392

TEC61392

TEC61392

Bugs Aplenty!

✂ Cut. 🧴 Glue.

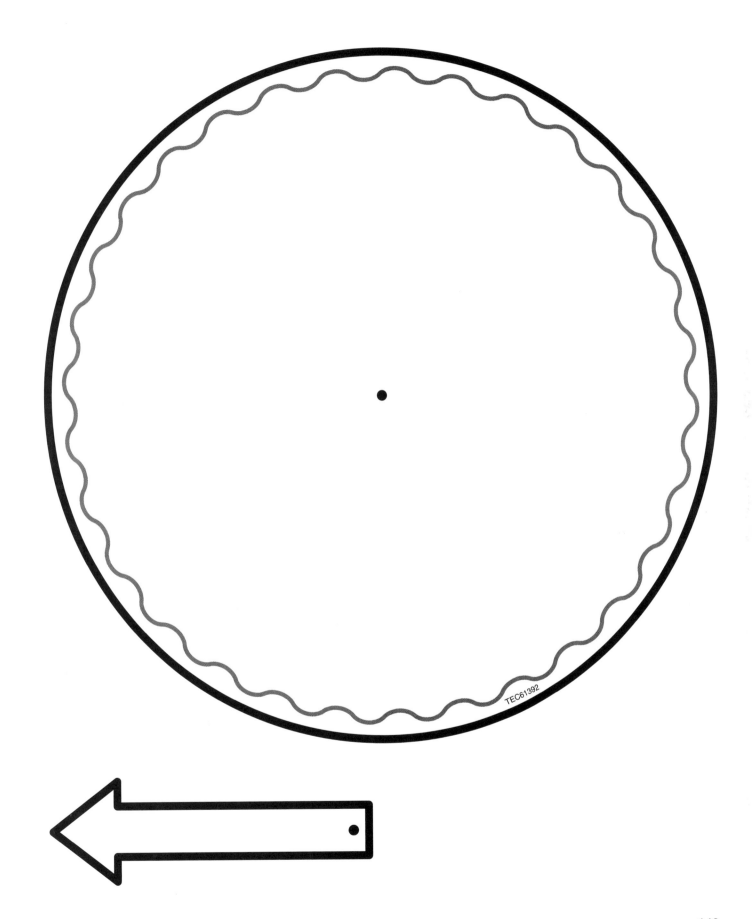

TEC61392

Counters

TEC61392   TEC61392   TEC61392   TEC61392

TEC61392   TEC61392   TEC61392   TEC61392

TEC61392   TEC61392   TEC61392   TEC61392

TEC61392   TEC61392   TEC61392   TEC61392

TEC61392   TEC61392   TEC61392   TEC61392

Day-by-Day Math Plans • ©The Mailbox® Books • TEC61392

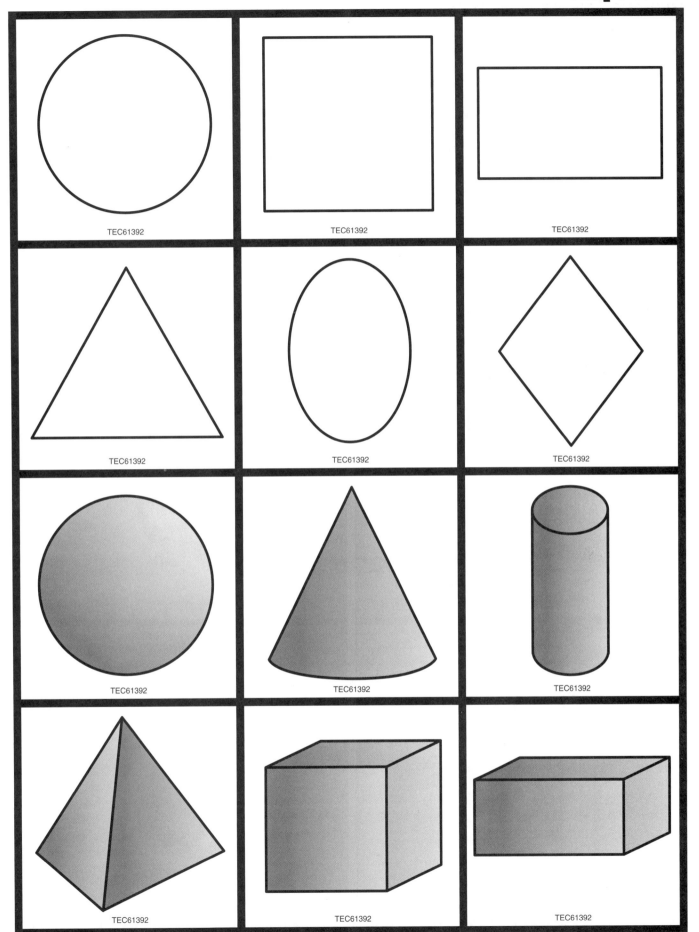

TEC61392

TEC61392

TEC61392

TEC61392

TEC61392

TEC61392

TEC61392

TEC61392

TEC61392

TEC61392

TEC61392

TEC61392

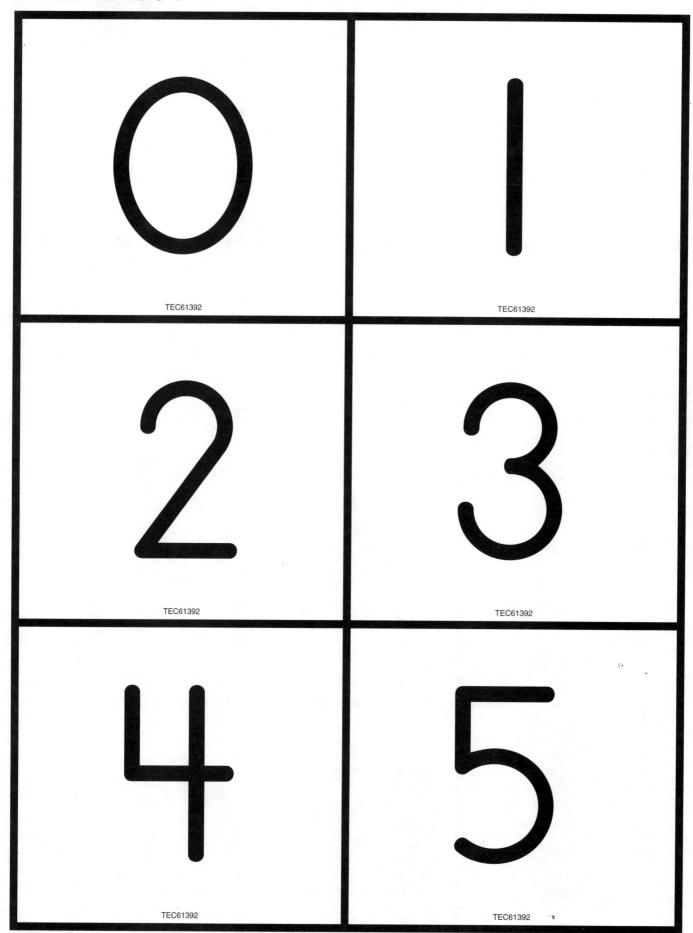

0 TEC61392

1 TEC61392

2 TEC61392

3 TEC61392

4 TEC61392

5 TEC61392

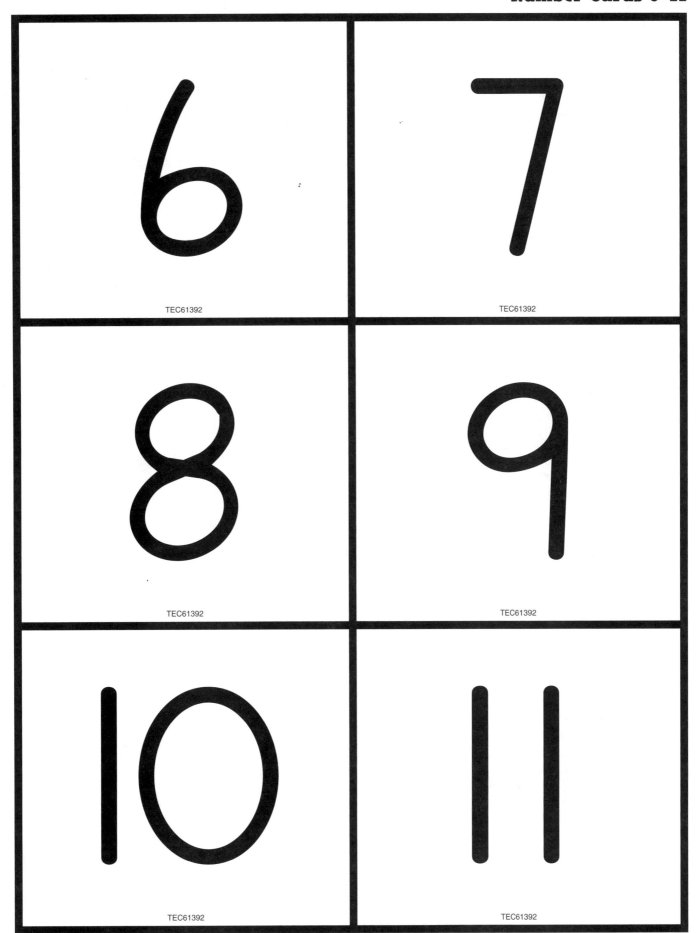

6 — TEC61392

7 — TEC61392

8 — TEC61392

9 — TEC61392

10 — TEC61392

11 — TEC61392

Number Cards 12–17

12 TEC61392	13 TEC61392
14 TEC61392	15 TEC61392
16 TEC61392	17 TEC61392

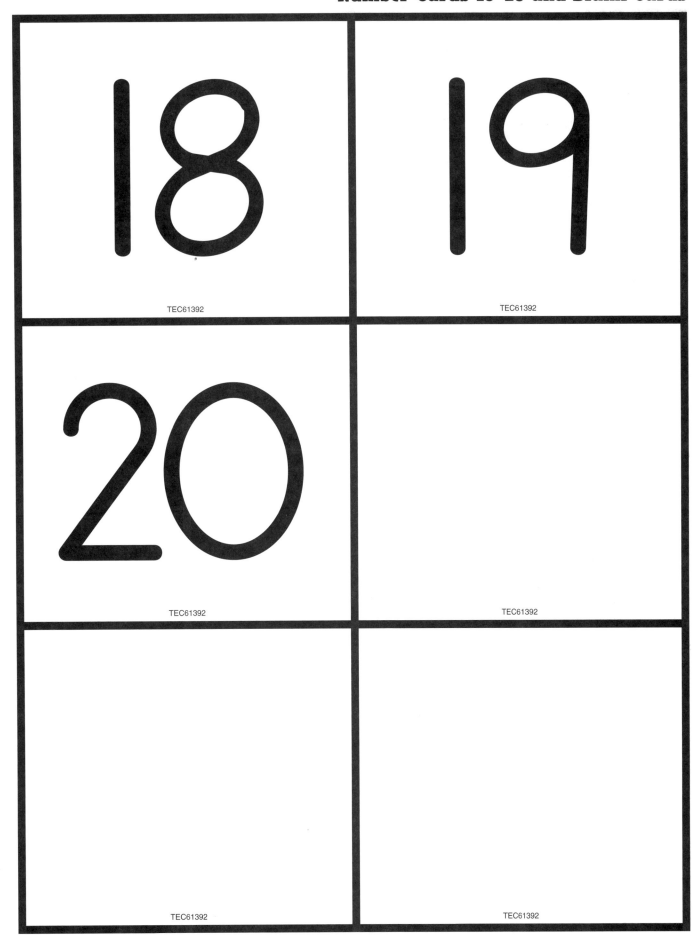

18

TEC61392

19

TEC61392

20

TEC61392

TEC61392

TEC61392

TEC61392

Sorting Mat: Two Sections

TEC61392

Sorting Mat: Two Sections

TEC61392

Assessment Checklist

LEARNING CENTER STARS

Name									
1.									
2.									
3.									
4.									
5.									
6.									
7.									
8.									
9.									
10.									
11.									
12.									
13.									
14.									
15.									
16.									
17.									
18.									
19.									
20.									
21.									
22.									
23.									
24.									
25.									
26.									
27.									
28.									
29.									
30.									

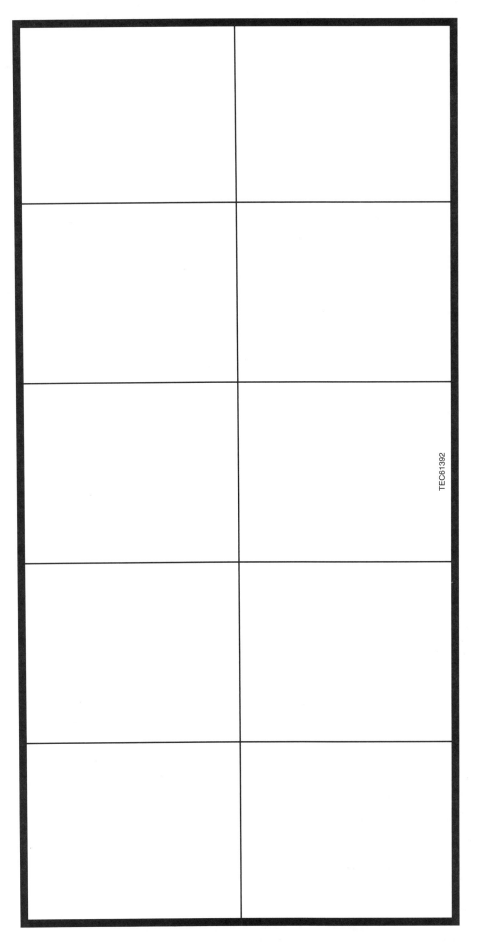

TEC61392

Blank Number Sentence Strips

TEC61392

TEC61392

TEC61392

TEC61392